Taunton Steam

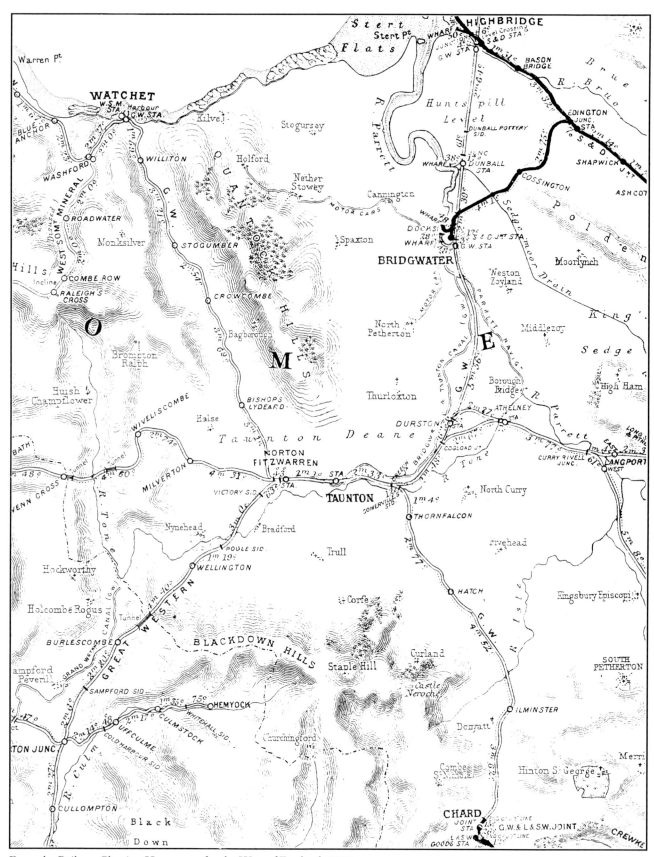

From the Railway Clearing House map for the West of England, 1918

Taunton Steam

Colin G Maggs

Millstream Books

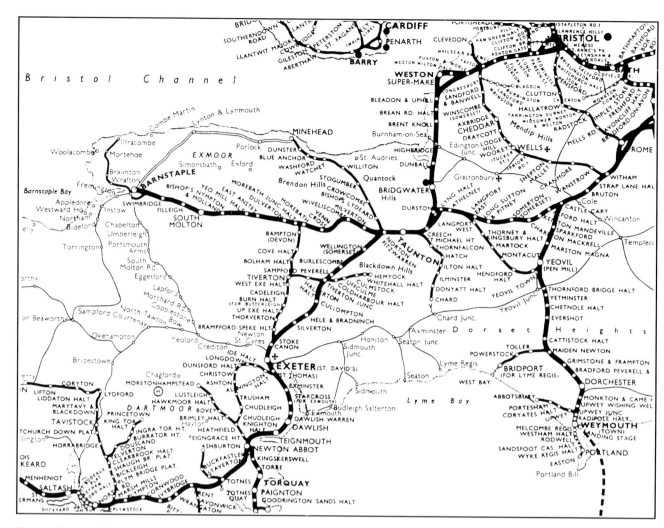

Extract from a GWR map, c.1930

First published 1991

Millstream Books
7 Orange Grove
Bath BA1 1LP

This book has been set in Janson Text by Ryburn Typesetting, Halifax
Printed in Great Britain by The Amadeus Press, Huddersfield

© Colin G Maggs 1991

ISBN 0 948975 26 1

Contents

	Introduction	6
Chapter 1	Taunton to Bridgwater	7
Chapter 2	Taunton to Wellington and Whiteball Tunnel	43
Chapter 3	Taunton to Langport West and Langport East	61
Chapter 4	Taunton to Thornfalcon	69
Chapter 5	Taunton to Milverton	75
Chapter 6	Taunton to Bishops Lydeard	79
Chapter 7	The Motive Power Scene: 1930s to 1960s	83
Chapter 8	Accidents and Mishaps	121
Chapter 9	Signalling	129
Chapter 10	The Goods Department at Taunton: 1930–1965	135
Chapter 11	Named Trains	147
Appendix	Locomotive Allocations	156
	Bibliography and Acknowledgments	160

GREAT WESTERN RAILWAY.

EXCURSION

FROM

LONDON TO BATH, BRISTOL, TAUNTON, AND EXETER, AND BACK,

On MONDAY, 2nd SEPTEMBER 1844, and following Days.

The DIRECTORS of the GREAT WESTERN RAILWAY have determined to afford to Persons desirous of visiting BATH, BRISTOL, TAUNTON, or EXETER, an opportunity of so doing by means of the following

EXCURSION TRAINS, AT REDUCED FARES:

SPECIAL TRAINS will leave London for Bath and Bristol on Monday, 2nd September, at 7 o'clock, A.M.; and on Friday, 6th September, at 3 o'clock P.M.; returning from Bristol and Bath to London, either on Wednesday, the 4th September, at Half-past 7 o'clock, A.M.; or on Saturday, the 7th September, at 4 o'clock, P.M.

SPECIAL TRAINS will leave Bath for Taunton and Exeter, calling at Bristol, and starting thence half an hour later on Tuesday, 3rd September, at 8 o'clock, A.M., and on Saturday, 7th September, at 5 o'clock, P.M.: returning from Exeter to Bristol and Bath either on Tuesday, 3rd September, at 4 o'clock, P.M., or on Friday, 6th September, at Half-past 7 o'clock, A.M.

The REDUCED FARES will be for these EXCURSION TRAINS:—

	1st Class.	2nd Class.
LONDON to BATH and Back / BATH to LONDON and Back	28s.	19s.
LONDON to BRISTOL and Back / BRISTOL to LONDON and Back	30s.	20s.
BRISTOL to EXETER and Back / EXETER to BRISTOL and Back	18s.	11s.
BATH to EXETER and Back / EXETER to BATH and Back	20s.	12s.

The Tickets will enable Passengers to travel by any of the Excursion Trains, Up or Down.

By this means, parties may travel from London to Exeter or Taunton, by taking the 7 A.M. Train from London, on the Monday, to Bristol; proceeding thence to Exeter or Taunton, on Tuesday morning. They can remain at these places until Friday morning, when they will return to Bristol, and reach London by the Saturday evening Train, from Bristol.

Further Particulars may be obtained by application at the Paddington, Exeter, Taunton, Bath, or Bristol Stations, where Tickets are to be obtained; and for any number exceeding twenty, taken by one individual, an allowance of 1s. per Ticket will be made.

An advertisement for the first special excursion trains run by the GWR

Introduction

Taunton was, and still is the centre of all the meadows, cornfields and orchards of the rich Vale of Taunton Deane. It is the county town of Somerset and a centre of education, with several boarding schools.

Regarding transport, by 1717 the River Tone had been made navigable to Taunton for barges carrying 15 tons. River traffic was superseded by the more direct Bridgwater & Taunton Canal in 1827, while the Grand Western Canal was extended to Tiverton in 1838, and in 1842 the Chard Canal branched off the Bridgwater & Taunton at Creech.

With the development of railways, Taunton, gateway to the south-west, had to be served because of the worthwhile traffic it would encourage. Once the first line was established, branches soon started to radiate from the town. Taunton became an important centre, there being no less than nine junctions within the district: Cogload, Creech, Durston, Athelney, Curry Rivel, Taunton East, Taunton West and the two at Norton Fitzwarren.

William Penny, a speculative builder, foreseeing Taunton as a growing rail centre and that railwaymen would need homes near the station, built a housing estate to the north-west in about 1892, a period of rapid population expansion. In due course, many of these dwellings were indeed occupied by railwaymen. He named the streets after his eight sons: Cyril, Fowler, Herbert, Maxwell, Raymond, Thomas, William and Leslie. Being a teetotaller, he built shops on the estate but no public house and placed a restrictive covenant on each dwelling that no licence to brew or sell alcohol would be applied for.

1831	1841	1851	1861	1871
11,139	12,066	13,319	13,720	15,466
1881	1891	1901	1911	1921
16,614	18,026	21,087	22,561	23,223
1931	1951	1961	1971	1981
25,178	33,620	35,192	37,444	35,482

Table showing the population of Taunton since 1831

Passenger traffic operation at Taunton, particularly on summer Saturdays from the 1930s onwards, presented a continuous spectacle with a wide variety of Great Western locomotive power. West Country expresses from and to Paddington, usually headed by a 'King' or 'Castle', were sometimes non-stop, or if calling, might well detach an Ilfracombe or Minehead portion needing subsequent marshalling and dispatch by branch train. North and West, Midland and South Wales services via Bristol were powered variously by 'Castle', 'Hall', 'Star' and 'Saint' classes, while the semi-fast and stopping trains to Bristol and Exeter were likewise provided for, plus the alternative of a 'Bulldog' or 43XX Mogul. Many other classes were to be seen on the branches to Yeovil, Chard, Barnstaple or Minehead, and on station duties. All contributed to the broad diversity of operation which gave Taunton its fascination.

Cyril Street, on William Penny's estate, forms the background to this derailment west of Taunton station in June 1947. 'Bulldog' No 3361 (Taunton) is being re-railed with assistance from tool van No 66 belonging to the Loco, Carriage & Wagon Department, Taunton.

Roger Venning

1. Taunton to Bridgwater

Even before the Great Western Railway Act was passed, a meeting was held at Taunton on the 24th February 1835 to consider linking the town with Bristol. Then in September, only a month after Royal Assent had been given to the GWR Act, Bristol merchants issued a prospectus for extending the broad gauge to Exeter. No time was lost, for within a month the estimated capital of £1.5m had been subscribed, a survey made and the necessary plans deposited. Like the GWR itself, the Bristol & Exeter Railway had I K Brunel as its engineer.

As with motorway construction today, the work was too great to be done as a single entity, but was opened in sections, the first being from Bristol to Bridgwater on 14th June 1841. Contracts for the length between Bridgwater and Taunton were let in the spring of 1841. Work proceeded quickly and the line opened on 1st July 1842. By 11.00am thousands of well-dressed people congregated along the railway, the *Somerset County Gazette* reporting:

> *At a quarter past eleven o'clock a long train of carriages were seen advancing a short distance from the terminus and in another moment a splendid engine named the 'Castor' with a long train of carriages "pulled up" before the station house.*

Somerset Bridge over the River Parrett, built of stone from a quarry near Langport, had a remarkably flat arch rising only 12 feet in its 100-ft span – even flatter than Brunel's more famous and severely criticised Maidenhead Bridge. Due to a slight movement of the foundations, he would not risk moving the timber centering supporting the masonry and when his Directors insisted on a replacement bridge, he retained the same abutments, but substituted a 102-ft span timber

arch which lasted for 61 years until renewed by one of a steel girder pattern, but still resting on Brunel's foundations. It was specially guarded in both World Wars as its destruction would have created a serious holdup in the flow of rail traffic.

At first the B&ER was worked by the GWR, but on 1st May 1849 the former took over operations using the existing Great Western staff, though from 1855, men employed in the goods department were the servants of the contractor J C Wall, and not directly employed by the company. The B&ER rifle green uniform was similar to that of the GWR, but with 'BER' on caps and collars.

Like the GWR, the B&ER carried a travelling porter in a hooded seat on the locomotive tender in order to keep a watch over the train to make sure nothing untoward happened to it, critics of the GWR and its associates referring to him has 'the man in the iron coffin'. Around 1854 this post was replaced by the cheaper expedient of raising a section of the guard's van roof and providing the guard with an elevated seat from which he could see forward and backward. So that he could communicate with the driver, a rope passed over the carriage roofs to operate the brake whistle on the engine. The B&ER was amalgamated with the GWR on 1st August 1876.

Durston station in broad gauge days, c.1865. A branch train from Yeovil is on the right; the main line to Bridgwater on the left; and the Railway Hotel far right. Notice, close to the foot of the telegraph pole, a capstan for moving the point blades and a target for indicating their position. *Edward Jebault Collection*

View towards Bristol from Creech St Michael, 1865. The track is on a very rigid frame: the rails are fixed to longitudinal beams held at the correct distance by cross pieces, while additional cross pieces link the Up and Down tracks. Ballast is packed under each longitudinal sleeper.
Edward Jeboult Collection

The B&ER was built to the broad gauge of 7 ft 0¼ in between the rails. In November 1867, Bridgwater to Durston had a third rail added to the narrower (standard) gauge of 4 ft 8½ ins, this mixed gauge being extended to Taunton in May 1875. The first standard gauge train reached Taunton on 30th May. On 18th June another standard gauge train conveyed implements from the North, Midlands and Eastern counties to the Royal Agricultural Society's showyard at Taunton. The following February mixed gauge was completed to Exeter, the *Somerset County Gazette* for 26th February 1876 reporting:

An experimental trip was made on Thursday by several leading officials of the Bristol & Exeter Railway for the purpose of testing the completeness and efficiency of the narrow gauge railway laid between Taunton and Exeter.

A new engine with two new carriages attached, conveyed the party, which consisted of Mr Walton, the Divisional Superintendent, Mr Cooper, Assistant Engineer, Mr Dunsford, Contractor, Mr Robinson, District Locomotive Superintendent, Mr Price Wall, Goods Manager, and Mr Gibson, General Superintendent at Taunton.

The various sidings and stations were put to a scrutinising test, and in every respect was most satisfactory. Now that the narrow gauge traffic has been rendered possible throughout the Great Western line and the main line of its recent acquisition, the Bristol & Exeter Railway, it has been proposed to bring that gauge into use on the 1st of March so far as the goods traffic is concerned.

This, it is expected, will confer a boon upon the agriculturalist of the west, it being contemplated to run a meat train into the Smithfield Market, thus saving the stoppage at the Paddington station and the expense of repacking and cartage.

The development of Taunton as a railway centre led to serious congestion and to ease the situation, the goods avoiding line was opened on 1st November 1896. This line was built approximately on the site of the Grand Western Canal. The waterway had been sold to the B&ER in 1864, the railway closing this section of the canal that same year. The goods avoiding line was a long time coming to fruition. As far back as 23rd December 1876 the *Somerset County Gazette* reported that a survey was being carried out for building a loop line south of the passenger station. This step had been recommended by Captain Tyler of the Board of Trade when he had inspected the newly-laid mixed gauge and expressed surprise at the great amount of traffic passing through the station. He strongly urged that an avoiding line should be built in order to keep goods trains away from what ought to be used only as a passenger station. The paper added:

There is, close to the down station, a piece of garden ground upon which it is proposed to erect a commodious Goods Shed and connect it by means of a loop line, running to Fairwater, with the main highway. It will be unnecessary to construct a bridge across Station Road as the old aqueduct can be utilised.

By the late 1920s, though, matters were as bad as ever, particularly on summer Saturdays. Most passenger trains called at Taunton, many having through coaches for Ilfracombe and Minehead which needed to be detached. As trains were following each other closely block by block, a small delay caused by an awkward coupling or corridor connection, caused hold-ups to snowball. Help was at hand in the form of the Development (Loans Guarantees & Grants) Act of 1929 which, with the aim of relieving national unemployment, provided funds for the improvement of large public works and Taunton station qualified for this.

Probably the most outstanding feature of the improvements was the quadrupling of tracks from Cogload Junction to Norton Fitzwarren, a distance of eight miles. It was important because it meant that the two Down routes – via Bristol and via Castle Cary – ceased to be interdependent, no longer having to approach Taunton

An extract from the B&ER timetable for January 1877

The goods avoiding line branches off to the left as No 7004 *Eastnor Castle* (Gloucester) accelerates with a Penzance to Manchester and Liverpool express in late February 1947. Although a late afternoon shot, frost still lies on the sleepers.   *Roger Venning*

No 6368 (Westbury) waiting on the goods loop by Taunton East Loop signalbox with a Down fast freight in March 1947.
Roger Venning

View Up: rebuilding Fairwater Bridge, Staplegrove, Taunton, in 1930 in preparation for quadrupling the track. The bridge was supplied by the Horseley Bridge & Engineering Co and some of the girders are so named. The steam crane carries the roughly printed warning 'Keep your eye open'.

S Bowditch Collection

station along the same line. Furthermore, the signalling of a Down train from Bristol would no longer delay an Up train to Castle Cary as the Down line from Bristol was carried over the Up and Down Castle Cary lines by a flying junction. The task of quadrupling involved the contractors Scott & Middleton in rebuilding 16 bridges and the removal of 140,000 cubic yards of earth. The work started in September 1930 and finished in April 1932.

Description of the line from Taunton to Bridgwater

As Taunton lay to the south of the Bristol & Exeter Railway, the original station was built by Brunel on the one-sided principle which he also adopted at Reading and Exeter, St David's. In order to avoid passengers having to cross the line, and to enable through trains to run clear of the platforms, Brunel created the startling innovation of having separate Up and Down stations on the same length of track and logically, the Up was at the London end of the layout. Each Up and Down station had its own office block constructed in a domestic style of architecture, the Up building being single-storey and the Down, two-storey.

Development of traffic caused the one-sided system to fall out of favour as an Up train crossing over to a platform could interfere with the movement of a Down train. The task of converting it to a conventional layout started in late April 1867. On 29th June 1867 the *Somerset County Gazette* reported:

The New Railway Station

Workmen have commenced the demolition of part of the present Down station, and the whole of the passenger traffic will be shortly conducted at the Up station, which has been temporarily enlarged for that purpose. Mr Douth of the Railway Hotel has erected a refreshment room on the extended platform. At the new station handsome refreshment rooms will be assigned to him, and he there will provide what has long been considered a desideratum by travellers on the Bristol and Exeter line.

The Down platform was lengthened to deal with longer trains, an Up platform built, and both covered by a train shed, a feature which the inhabitants of a town of any standing considered obligatory. The work of enlargement was completed on 17th August 1868, the *Somerset County Gazette* for 22nd August commenting:

Railway Station, Taunton.

Watercolour by H Frier of the Up station, Taunton, 1855.

Taunton passenger staff outside the former Down line station building, 1885.

J F King Collection

Pre-1931 view inside the train shed showing a slip coach standing at platform 1.

GWR

Taunton Railway Station

The new Taunton Railway station was opened for traffic on Monday morning. A large number of detonating signals announced the arrivals of the first up and down trains, and the arrangements appear to be, as proved by the past week's experience, in every respect perfect. The works have been in hand more than a twelve month, and it was expected that all would have been completed last Spring, but as several extras have been added to the items contained in the original contract, the finishing touches had to be postponed. The people of Taunton, however much they may have grumbled at having to put up so long with an inconvenient makeshift, may now be fairly satisfied with the additional accommodation the providing of which caused the delay. When a quarter of a century ago, the old station was first opened, and the novel sound of the locomotives' asthmatic shriek ran through the valley, it must have been a far seeing person to have predicted not only such an increase in traffic on the main line as has taken place, but the growth of branches North and South, making Taunton a railway centre, and rendering the provision of a suitable station an absolute necessity. Mindful of the recent wakefulness of the shareholders as regards expenditure, the company have only done justice to the importance of our county town, wasting no money in mere ornamentation, and

making available, as far as possible, the materials of the old, down station. Approaching the new erection from the Taunton side, the building looks substantial and well proportioned – almost elegant. Wings of offices and waiting and refreshment rooms extend on each side of the old square block of building, the elevation of which is embellished by a glazed verandah. Above the Bath stone cornices rises the long slated roof with its "capping of glass", the apex 42' above the ground. The total length of the station under the roof is 250'. The skylight is 200' in length and its slope on each side gives a breadth of 28'. The width of the roof within the walls is 88'. Suspended from the gigantic cobweb of standards and braces which supports the roof are half a hundred or so of globe-shaped lamps whose long rows of lights at night produce a pretty effect. Return walls at the ends of the covered platforms, with triangular glazed windows spreading downwards from the extremities of the roof ridge a distance of 18', will help to afford shelter from the rain and wind. After crowding on a narrow wooden strip, it is pleasant to pace unjostled, unalarmed by the cry "By yr leave", the broad expanses of Pennant stone. On the down side (nearest to Taunton) the platform is 21' wide and 540' long – 250' within the walls, 60' outside towards Bristol, and 230' over the bridge (where it narrows) in the direction of Wellington. It is from this part of the platform that the Watchet trains will start.

Dragon at Taunton hauling the last Down broad gauge express on 20th May 1892. Note the platform extension outside the train shed, and the engine shed roof beyond *Dragon's* chimney.
J F King Collection

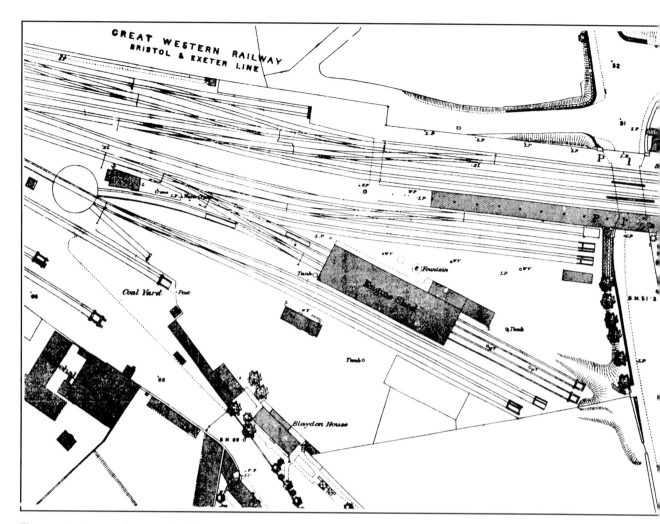

Taunton station on a large-scale Ordnance Survey map of 1888

On the up side the platform is still wider, 28' 8",
extending beyond the roof at the Western extremity 33'
(to the bridge over the road) and at the opposite end
60'. Here a dock is cut out 120' long for the
accommodation of the Chard trains; and into this the
trains from Watchet are shunted. The three lines of
rails between the main platforms are spanned by an
iron bridge 7½' wide, to which a double flight of stone
steps about the same width of the bridge lead up at each
end. The Superintendent's apartments, parcels office,
and refreshment rooms are on the down side platform.
On both the up and down sides are booking offices and
waiting rooms, comfortably fitted up. We believe there
was slight difficulty at first as to securing an approach
from Kingston road to the up platform, and when the
depth of the cutting, and height and solidity of the walls
are regarded, it will be seen that to carry out this
excellent addenda involved considerable labour and
expense. If not now a necessity, it is certainly a
convenience the company have done well to secure.
When the road at that part is well worn it will look
better than it does now. The short cut for foot
passengers to the down station, by the side of the hotel,

must also be put, and kept, in good order. We would
suggest whether the positioning of the directing board
at the corner of the enclosure just beyond the canal
bridge makes it as intelligible a guide as it might be.
These, and other smaller matters to be, probably
hereafter discovered and rectified, will make our new
station all that it can be made.

The general impression produced by the building is
that it is conveniently planned and efficiently carried
out by the contractors (Messrs Brock and Company of
Bristol).

In 1895 the platforms were further extended, that on
the Up side taking in the goods shed site and giving
Taunton the honour of having the longest platforms on
the Great Western system. Bay platforms were added at
each end of the main platforms to deal with terminating
trains and thereby keep them from delaying those on the
through roads. By this time train sheds were falling from
favour, so the bays were protected by cheaper platform
awnings supported on pylon-type columns. In 1907, to
accommodate new, wider engines, the Down road was
moved out a little and, as it proved impossible to move

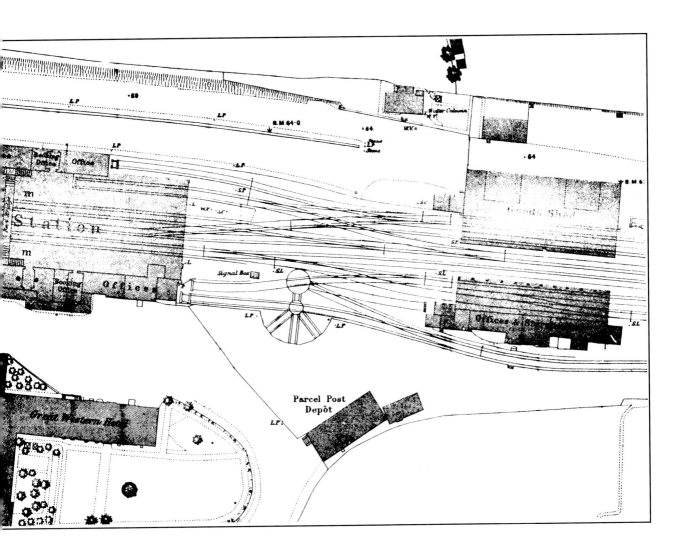

the Up line, two inches of the platform stonework was removed.

With quadrupling, the train shed was demolished and replaced with four through, and five bay platforms, the former varying from 1400 ft to 1200 ft (contemporary passenger coaches varied from 60–70 ft in length). Alterations involved widening and lengthening by 50 ft the bridge carrying the railway over Station Road. As the flying junction at Cogload caused the Castle Cary lines to be the centre tracks, main line trains via this route tended to use the island platforms, Bristol trains using the outer roads. The Down bay 2 was used mainly by Chard trains, one leaving for this branch blocking both Down lines, and if routed on the relief line, the Up main line as well. Down bay platforms 3 & 4 were for trains to Barnstaple, Minehead and some Exeter stopping trains. Platform 8 was used almost exclusively for arrivals from Barnstaple and Minehead, though it was also signalled for departures. Platform 9 was used by trains to Bristol and Yeovil.

The improvements of the 1930s involved replacing the footbridge by a subway 140 ft long and 15 ft wide. This came into use on 17th January 1932 and the pleasant contemporary bronze hoods over the lamps at the foot of the stairways are still in place. At the north end of the subway a new booking hall was built. The remodelled station was completed on 20th December 1931.

During World War Two nearly all trains stopping at Taunton used platforms 1 or 7, staff being in short supply. Non-stop trains such as the 'Cornish Riviera Express' and the hundreds of troop trains which just halted for a crew change and water, and for the troops to be fed from food trolleys, used platforms 5 & 6. At the start of the war, the Church Army built a kitchen and canteen on the taxi rank outside the Down platform. Normally staffed by members of the Church Army, the Women's Voluntary Service also helped when needed. Trolleys of hot food were taken via the subway to the troop trains. In the British Railways era, passenger trains to and from Bristol used platforms 1 & 7 and those via Somerton 5 & 6. Until the end of steam an 80 mph limit was imposed through the station, but as most passenger trains stopped at Taunton, generally only the 'Cornish Riviera' and 'Torbay Express' ran through at this speed and gave onlookers a very exciting experience.

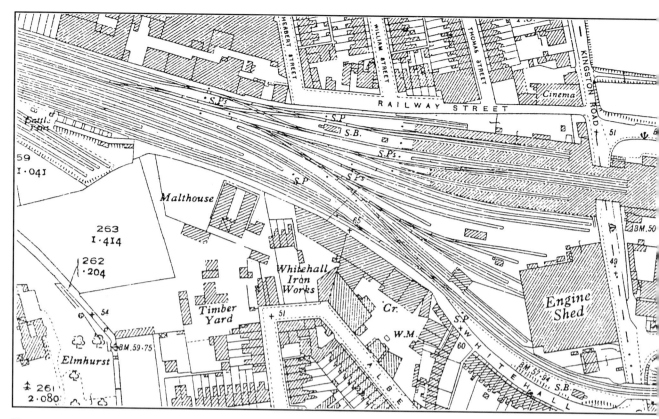

Taunton station on a 25-inch Ordnance Survey map of 1930

Taunton station: extension of the main line platforms at the west end and the addition of extra bay platforms, July 1895. The girders for the umbrella roof can be seen. The train shed is on the left, and the old engine shed, rebuilt the following year, right.

J F King Collection

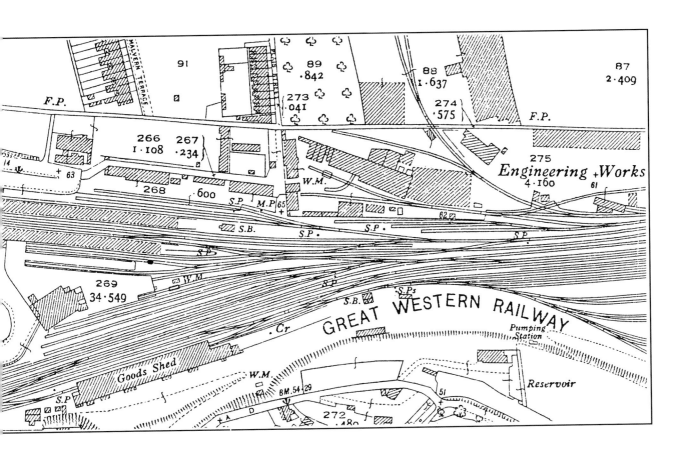

View Down, c.1905: East Station signalbox is on the right and the Station Hotel can be seen on the far left. *Lens of Sutton*

Some of the platform staff, c.1920, photographed on the Down platform.

J F King Collection

Taunton telegraph office staff outside their office in the 1920s.

J F King Collection

Aerial view, c.1927: the goods shed and goods loop are at the lower left and William Penny's estate upper left.   *Author's Collection*

1931 booking hall viewed from the Up side station approach road.   *Author's Collection*

Station yard, c.1953, and the office building which was formerly the Down station. *Lens of Sutton*

0-6-0PT No 9671 stands at platform 7 with express headlights, probably adding vehicles to an Up express, c.1950. A Down train of ex-LMS stock stands in platform 1. Notice the large nameboard giving extensive information. *Lens of Sutton*

Aerial view, c.1960, looking east. The large square building south of the station is the loco depot. The goods shed can be seen to the south-east of the curving approach road, on the Down side of the passenger station.   *J F King Collection*

Taunton nameboard, 1st September 1962.   *S P J A Derek*

With the withdrawal of branch services following the implementation of the Beeching Plan, some platforms proved surplus to requirements and so to economise on maintenance, the island platforms were taken out of use, though not in fact until 31st March 1976, lines serving them henceforth being used by through non-stop trains. The structures on those platforms were subsequently removed and advertisement hoardings placed facing the seats on the outer platforms, but elsewhere trees have been planted. In the event of an emergency, access to the island platforms is still possible by stairs from the subway. The three platforms remaining in use have been re-numbered: 1 Down; 2 Up; and 3 Up bay, the latter used for the departure of trains for Bristol which have previously terminated at the station.

On 16th March 1983 a new booking office and travel centre was opened, the building virtually obscuring the façade of the 1931 booking hall. This move almost completely reversed conditions of the 1840s – then the station was on the south side; today, although the south side entrance remains, passengers entering that side have to walk across to the north in order to purchase a ticket. The station brickwork was cleaned in the 1980s, giving it a fresh appearance.

No 4089 *Donnington Castle* (Bristol, Bath Road) leaves platform 7 with an Up express, 15th September 1946. *Pursey Short*

Through platform 1, 1st June 1946: No 6004 *King George III* (Plymouth, Laira) being oiled by the driver while the fireman shovels coal forward to a more accessible position before leaving with a Paddington to Penzance express. In bay platform 3, No 5999 *Wollaton Hall* (Taunton) awaits departure with a Taunton to Exeter stopping train. *Roger Venning*

The driver of 'County' No 1011, later named *County of Chester*, has just finished oiling his 5-month old locomotive before leaving with a Penzance to Manchester express composed of very assorted coaches, 2nd June 1946. One inspection pit can be seen on the left at the end of platform 6, while another is in front of No 1011 standing at platform 7. A 'devil' for ensuring that the water crane did not freeze is visible on the right hand edge of the picture. *Roger Venning*

No 2214 (Taunton) in bay platform 3 heading a Taunton to Barnstaple train in July 1947. Far right, No 4113 (Taunton) on a Minehead train in bay platform 4.
Roger Venning

'County' No 1014 (Bristol, Bath Road), still awaiting naming, at platform 5 by Taunton West Station signalbox on 10th June 1946. Notice the Automatic Train Control ramp in the foreground.
Roger Venning

Through platform 5: No 5071 *Spitfire* (Newton Abbot) heads a Bristol to Kingswear express on 6th July 1946. Note the inset doors on the wide-bodied first coach. *Roger Venning*

Braziers provided at the water columns to prevent them from freezing were known to footplatemen as 'devils' and when in use, it was the responsibility of a couple of engine cleaners or 'spare' firemen to maintain a supply of coal and to remove any ashes to the engine shed for subsequent disposal. It was quite an arduous task wheeling a barrow-load of coal from the shed to the more remote columns.

Pits were provided between the running lines at the ends of the platforms to enable enginemen to check the underside of their locomotive and were especially useful for inspecting the valve gear which was generally situated between the frames of a GWR engine.

The carriage sidings at the east end of the station stabled coaches for stopping trains to Bristol and als spares. Branch line passenger trains usually consisted of at least one 'B' non-corridor set and one or two corrido thirds. A stock of carriages was also kept in the carriag sidings at the west end of the station for strengthenin main line or branch trains. The short spur situated at th east end of the station between the Up and Down mai lines was used during summer working for stablin locomotives awaiting the arrival of Up through train from the Barnstaple and Minehead branches, or fo holding parcel vans awaiting attachment to Up parcel trains. Additionally it was used for accommodatin wagons with hot axle boxes which needed to be remove from Up goods trains.

Through platform 7: photographer Roger Venning stands on platform 6 admiring No 5076 *Gladiator* (Bristol, Bath Road) with West to North express composed of London & North Eastern Railway coaches on 21st June 1946. Notice the pit between the track at the end of platform 6 to allow access to the inside motion of a locomotive. This facility was only provided at some principa stations. On either side of the pit, the track is laid on longitudinal, not cross, sleepers. *Pursey Shor*

A Taunton to Bristol stopping train waits to leave platform 7 behind No 4099 *Kilgerran Castle* (Newton Abbot) on 8th April 1950. Notice the 'devil' with two chimneys at the top, placed to prevent the water crane freezing.   *Pursey Short*

There was a Wyman's bookstall on Taunton station and the manager, William Vincent, was highly efficient as can be noticed from the following extracts of his *Seen from a Railway Platform* published in 1919:

Owing to the delay of parcels containing library-books from London, I was unable one day to send books to a twelve-volume subscriber some miles out of Taunton by a weekly carrier, so after business in the evening, I took the 7.40 train to Wellington (Somerset) station … and walked the remaining five miles with the books. In returning to Wellington I found the last train back had been gone some time, therefore I put up at the White Horse Inn *but thinking the bed damp, I slept in my overcoat and was up early the next morning for the first train. This was much better than keeping a client waiting a whole week until the carrier's next journey. Indeed I didn't mind a journey like this now and then, even, as in the present case, at my own expense.*

In 1935 the Taunton stationmaster was Mr Morrish who previously had occupied the same position at Minehead. On the station staff was Chief Inspector Hutchings, a most imposing character of very upright and clean appearance, always displaying the customary button hole. He was assisted by three inspectors on the Down side and three on the Up. The yardmaster was Arthur Aplin, stockily built, with bushy moustache, and with a voice like a bullhorn. He could stand outside his office and shout to a foreman shunter, making his voice carry over the noise of a shunting engine. He was also a JP and local councillor. His office was in a line of buildings alongside the vehicular road to the mileage yard office. Next door was the yard inspector's office, and beyond, the crew rooms and the carriage & wagon staff. A former lad messenger recalls that he used to enjoy visiting the inspector's office about 9.00am and being greeted by the delicious aroma of frying bacon plus the added smells of steam locomotives and axle grease! The

No 5944 *Ickenham Hall* (Wolverhampton, Stafford Road) enters platform 1 with a Down express, 4th May 1946. The yard inspector's office is to the right of the locomotive's chimney. *Pursey Short*

number of staff employed by the GWR at Taunton peaked at around 1800 in 1943.

At the east end of the station is the concrete depot. Originated by the GWR, it began in a small way in 1898 and has continued under BR, from 1963 also taking over work performed by a similar depot set up by the London & South Western Railway at Exmouth Junction, Exeter. It provided such items as fence and loading gauge posts, paving stones, signalbox coal bins and, during World War Two, 'pot' type concrete sleepers for use in sidings, goods loops and branch lines to conserve timber sleepers for main lines where speeds were higher. In more recent years the depot has produced full length concrete sleepers and bridge sections, the former being cast around rods in tension; after three to four days drying, the wires were cut.

The Chard branch diverged at Creech Junction. The main line beyond burrowed beneath the Chard Canal. As the sub-strata was a deep clay bed, Brunel constructed a brick invert with retaining walls 660 yds long, in the centre of which was the aqueduct for carrying the canal. The railway descended into this invert at either end on a gradient varying from 1 in 250 to 1 in 300. Because of this dip, water collected under the aqueduct and had to be pumped into surface drains. Although the aqueduct was abolished in 1869, the B&ER having purchased the waterway two years previously, the invert was not filled and the line raised until 1895.

Creech St Michael halt, built at a cost of about £600, had a neat brick-built waiting room, and, unlike most halts, was staffed and had carefully-tended flower beds featured in the *Great Western Railway Magazine*.

A Down heavy goods train hauled by oil-burning 2-8-0 No 4807 (Plymouth, Laira) near Creech St Michael, 12th September 1947.

Pursey Short

Creech St Michael, view Down, with paper works in the distance, 21st August 1962.

Author

Beyond, Charlton Engine House was situated between the Bridgwater & Taunton Canal and the River Tone. This three-storey brick building erected in 1827, housed a seven-foot throw beam pump capable of 13 strokes a minute and worked by a low-pressure condensing engine. It could raise three and a half million gallons a day and kept the canal supplied with all water necessary for navigation. In August 1901 it was replaced by two locomotive boilers working a centrifugal pump capable of delivering 125,000 gallons an hour.

In 1902 Creech Troughs, 560 yds long, were opened to enable locomotives to replenish supplies in order to make non-stop runs between Paddington and Exeter. As the canal was at a slightly higher level than the railway, the troughs were filled by gravity, water flowing via a Float House built beside the original canal pumping station. The Float House contained two large floats – one for the Up lines and another for the Down. The Up relief and Up main line troughs were connected so that when water was taken from, say, the Up main, water flowed from the Up relief troughs to partly replenish it. Likewise the Down main and Down relief were interconnected.

As well as this extra supply of canal water – 54 locomotives used the troughs daily in 1904 – at this period the GWR also scoured out its dock at Bridgwater more frequently (41 extra times in addition to the normal 26 annual scourings), thus saving work with the mud-scraper boat. Each scouring used some four to five million gallons of canal water.

This extra water consumption would not have been criticised had it all been lifted from the Tone to the canal by the pump at Creech, but in order to avoid the cost of pumping, the railway company admitted water directly to the canal at Firepool Weir, next to Taunton station, where the canal was about 1 ft 4 ins below the normal level of the river. This seriously reduced the flow of water to Bathpool Mill and Ham Mill set between Taunton and Creech. Additionally the GWR pumping station at Firepool was abstracting 980,000 gallons a week in 1904 for locomotive and station purposes, whereas 20 years previously, consumption had only been 300,000 gallons. Until 1889 water was raised at Taunton station by hot air engines with a pump capacity of 8,000 gallons per hour, but that year they were replaced by a pair of steam pumps with a total capacity of just under 18,000 gallons an hour. The opening of Creech Troughs reduced the need for pumping at Taunton by four to five hours daily, but the outcome of this vast extraction of water from the Tone was that the mill owners and local farmers sought an injunction to restrain the GWR's usage. The case was brought before Bristol Summer Assize on 15th and 16th July 1904 when the GWR was held liable for damages.

No 3440 *City of Truro* with an Up express on Creech Troughs.

the late W Bras.

No 7014 *Caerhays Castle*, heading a Down express, passes the pumping station and float house for Creech Troughs on 5th August 1961.
John Cornelius

No 4919 *Donnington Hall*, near Creech, working empty milk tanks from Kensington to St Erth on 5th August 1961. *John Cornelius*

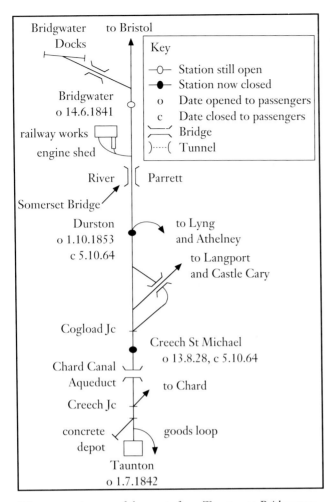

Key

○ Station still open
● Station now closed
o Date opened to passengers
c Date closed to passengers
⌒ Bridge
)····(Tunnel

Bridgwater Docks — to Bristol

Bridgwater
o 14.6.1841

railway works

engine shed

River) (Parrett

Somerset Bridge

Durston
o 1.10.1853
c 5.10.64

to Lyng
and Athelney

to Langport
and Castle Cary

Cogload Jc

Creech St Michael
o 13.8.28, c 5.10.64

Chard Canal
Aqueduct

Creech Jc

to Chard

concrete
depot

goods loop

Taunton
o 1.7.1842

Diagrammatic map of the route from Taunton to Bridgwater

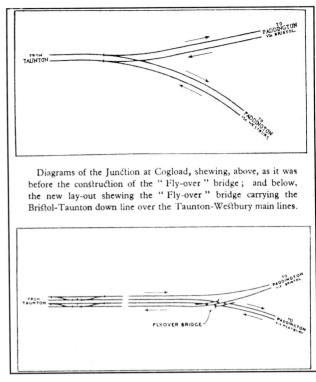

Diagrams of the Junction at Cogload, shewing, above, as it was before the construction of the " Fly-over " bridge ; and below, the new lay-out shewing the " Fly-over " bridge carrying the Bristol-Taunton down line over the Taunton-Westbury main lines.

Cogload flyover, from *Track Topics* (GWR, 1935)

The Bridgwater and Castle Cary lines diverged at Cogload Junction. Like the Somerset Bridge, this was protected by the Home Guard before D-Day in case the track and flying junction were destroyed by enemy agents anxious to delay the invasion.

A Paddington to Taunton via Bristol express climbing to the Cogload Junction flyover in 1938, hauled by No 5042 *Winchester Castle* It carried express headlights to Weston-super-Mare, then the stopping headcode for the journey on to Taunton.   *Bob Franklin*

No 4042 *Prince Albert* and No 3443 *Chaffinch*, (the latter of Taunton shed and driven by Reg Chudleigh, father of Bob, the former Taunton fireman who provided much information for this book), which had replaced a failed 'King'. They are seen passing Cogload Junction under the Down line from Bristol with the 8.30am Plymouth to Paddington express on 11th September 1947. *Pursey Short*

Durston Junction was where the branch to Athelney and Yeovil left the Bridgwater line. In its early days the Down platform, of island pattern, was narrow and had a train shed covering the branch line, but following the abolition of the broad gauge, the shed was removed and the platform widened. An unusually wide signalbox extended right across it. The turntable, taken out of use on 21st September 1952, was little used latterly. One driver taking an ammunition train from Bridgwater to Exeter during World War Two, as his engine was going bunker-first, turned it at Durston to ensure a more comfortable ride.

A Paddington to Bristol to Plymouth express, hauled by No 1014 *County of Glamorgan* (Bristol, Bath Road), hurries through Durston on 14th April 1949, while 0-6-0PT No 4689 (Yeovil) waits with a Yeovil to Taunton goods in the loop platform. *Pursey Short*

Durston: 2-6-2T No 4593 and 0-6-0PT No 9663 head a Locomotive Club of Great Britain special off the Yeovil branch on 16th February 1964. *Hugh Ballantyne*

The 9.35am Wolverhampton to Penzance, hauled by No 1005 *County of Devon* (Bristol, Bath Road), passes the water tank and arm of the setting down post for the single line token for trains coming off the branch from Athelney. View taken on 28th May 1950 at the north end of Durston station. *Pursey Short*

Oil-burning No 3952 *Norcliffe Hall* (Old Oak Common) heads a Paddington to Bristol to Taunton express on 3rd August 1947 just north of Durston.

Pursey Short

The low-lying stretch of line between Durston and Bridgwater was often subject to flooding. On 20th November 1875 an extra engine was coupled either at Durston or Bridgwater and, by accumulating steam and running very slowly, they could draw the train through, though on arrival steam was just about exhausted, the engines' fires having being doused by the time they reached dry ground. It took about nine minutes to pass through the floodwater one and a half miles long and 3 ft deep. It was a similar story a year later when water 5 ft 3 ins deep covered the line for five weeks and again a pilot engine was required. On this occasion only the parapet rail of the bridge over the River Parrett was visible above the water.

No 7011 *Banbury Castle* (Bristol, Bath Road), painted in an experimental apple-green livery, heads a Wolverhampton to Kingswear express near Somerset Bridge, Bridgwater on 19th February 1949. The six centre coaches are ex-LMS vehicles. Notice the gangers' trolley beside the track.
Pursey Short

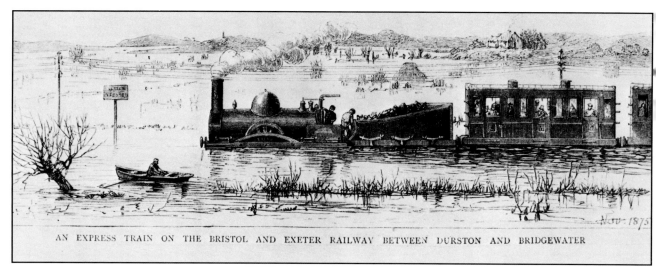

AN EXPRESS TRAIN ON THE BRISTOL AND EXETER RAILWAY BETWEEN DURSTON AND BRIDGEWATER

An express train passing through floods between Durston and Bridgwater, November 1875. *Author's Collection*

A 2-4-0T with water to footplate level, passing through floods at Creech with an Up train, c.1887. Notice the windmill, left, with paper mill beyond.
Author's Collection

Just south of Bridgwater station were the Carriage & Wagon Shops founded by the B&ER and once one of the town's major employers. On one occasion, employees did not see eye to eye with management, the *Weston Mercury* of 16th October 1886 reporting:

Working men held a demonstration on the Cornhill, Bridgwater, Saturday 9th October in the evening. The steam whistle known as "The Hooter", used at the GWR carriage works in the town for many years past and heard for a good distance, was a good timekeeper. Influential parties asked the GWR to discontinue it and it was, the previous Monday.

The working classes agitated for its continuance as the majority of firms in the town and district accepted it as their regular times for meals. The mayor admitted that it was he who had complained about it being blown unnecessarily long in the early morning. Then understanding the strong feelings of the working classes, he had since written asking that it continued to be blown. It was stated at the meeting on Saturday the 9th that another and larger hooter had been sent from Swindon to replace the one removed.

At the meeting were several hundred workers with a band, torches, flags and banners.

During the 1930s the works changed over to tarpaulin sheet examination and in World War Two all types of military canvas from tents to stretchers were repaired there. Eventually returned to civilian use, these works in Colley Lane caught fire early on 25th August 1947, the whole town being illuminated by the flames. Around 1500 sheets and hundreds of pulley blocks were lost in the blaze and the works never re-opened.

The main GWR sheet shop for manufacturing these articles for use on railway wagons and road lorries was at Worcester, Bridgwater having one of the subsidiary shops which merely examined and repaired them. Taunton made a daily return of wagons, sheets and ropes. This was sent to Exeter by train about 1.00pm, then about 3.30 to 4.00pm, instructions were received by wire for their disposal, faulty sheets being set aside and sent to Bridgwater. Until the 1940s sheets travelled in a station truck either to the Bridgwater depot or to a station which required them. Each sheet was numbered and every rope had a metal ferrule with a number. Every few years, at a given weekend, a census was taken of sheets, ropes and wagons on all railways, including private sidings, and submitted to the Railway Clearing House.

In addition to the B&ER Carriage & Wagon Works, in the middle of the last century there used also to be

Bristol & Exeter Railway's carriage works, Bridgwater, 1865, with traverser rails behind the entrance gates. The foreman wears a top hat.
P J Squibbs Collection

Bridgwater station, 1897, view Up. Note the change in the platform facing from stone to brick, indicating where it has been lengthened.

Hennet & Company, wagon builders and general engineers. This firm was taken over by the Bridgwater Engineering Co Ltd which ceased trading in 1878–9.

Bridgwater station is a fine Grade II listed building, designed by I K Brunel with matching buildings on both platforms. Of single-storey construction, it has deep Georgian style windows below a cornice, while the low-pitched roof is hidden behind a parapet. The walls are rendered in light stucco. In 1882, £3700 was spent on improvements – the platforms were extended by 15 ft, glazed roofs were added, as were waiting rooms and a new footbridge. The platforms were further extended in 1904.

One interesting dispatch from Bridgwater was elvers, merchants in Gloucester often demanding as much as a on a day. In the 1950s the goods department was very busy, employing about 50 men, the Bridgwater goods agent being graded higher than many of the Divisional staff. The yard is still open and a 50-ton crane lifts Hinkley Point power station containers.

From the goods yard a line led to a wharf on the River Parrett. This link had been opened by Bridgwater Corporation in 1845 as a horse tramway known as the 'Communication Works' and leased by the B&ER in August 1859, purchased by them in 1863 and four years later converted to mixed gauge and worked by locomotives. Four years later again, it was extended to the Docks. Its opening ended the practice of coal being

brought to Taunton by the Bridgwater & Taunton Canal and then distributed onwards by rail, as it could now be distributed direct from Bridgwater by rail without any additional transhipment.

This extension to the Docks entailed a bridge having to be built over the Parrett and to avoid interfering with river traffic, one of the spans was made telescopic. The bridge was divided into three sections and this sequence was followed to open it. The signals at each end of the bridge were placed at danger and a steel arm locked across the rails, thus physically preventing trains from trying to pass and 'commit suicide'. Gates across the footbridge and rail tracks were locked. Safety precautions having been taken, the first section was moved sideways, on wheels and special rails. The second section, (which spanned most of the river), was moved lengthways into the space vacated by the first section, thus allowing vessels to pass. The third section remained fixed. The two mobile sections were moved by a stationary steam engine. On one occasion in 1913 when the engine failed, the bridge was across the river. As it was imperative that it be opened, gangers operated it with ropes. Due to the upper berths on the river falling out of use, it is believed that the bridge was not opened after 1948.

Speed over the Docks branch was restricted to 5 mph and to guard against mishaps when crossing five public roads, a shunter and two hand-signalmen were required to accompany every trip. The line closed in April 1967.

A Bristol to Taunton stopping train leaves Bridgwater in 1938 behind No 4945 *Milligan Hall*.   *Bob Franklin*

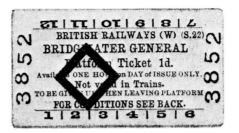

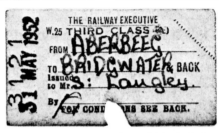

Bridgwater station, 1859, showing the staff outside the booking office: a signalman, centre, wears a top hat and with him are three porters and a lad porter.

P J Squibbs Collection

2. Taunton to Wellington and Whiteball Tunnel

The B&ER extended its line from Taunton through Wellington to a temporary terminus at Beam Bridge on 1st May 1843, Whiteball Tunnel being incomplete and needing another year's work. Pending its completion, stage coaches carried passengers on to Exeter. Beam Bridge was quite a busy terminus, enjoying a daily service of eight passenger and two goods trains until its closure on 1st May 1844 when the B&ER was opened throughout to Exeter. The railway staff at Beam Bridge was not renowned for its enthusiasm, porters being reluctant to meet stages coaches to unload baggage; then when they had glued labels on, they left the luggage on barrows instead of loading it on trains. To add to the confusion, the ticket office windows used to shut several minutes before a train left, causing some passengers to miss it.

'County' class No 1001, un-named, (Newton Abbot), climbs towards Whiteball Tunnel with a Down express, 20th July 1946.
Pursey Short

Description of the line from Taunton to Whiteball Tunnel

Leaving Taunton passenger station, the goods loop avoiding the platforms came in on the Down side at Taunton West yard. Beyond was the seven-road Fairwater yard built early in World War Two and from 1960 used by the Chief Civil Engineer for assembling and loading track. The sidings were worked by PWM (Permanent Way Maintenance) No 652, a diesel-electric 0-6-0 built by Ruston & Hornsby in 1959.

Immediately west of Silk Mill crossing, a siding to a sugar beet factory was opened on 29th August 1929 which 13 years later became Blinkhorn Sidings serving the United States Army stores. These were taken over in 1946 to become No 3 Supply Reserve Depot and worked by standard Ministry of Defence Army Department locomotives. The main depot closed in 1966, the site now being a trading estate.

On Saturday 29th June 1946, No 6023 *King Edward II* (Newton Abbot) heads an Up express between Fairwater Bridge and Forty Steps Bridge. On the right, 'Bulldog' No 3361 shunts coaches, while on the left a 54XX 0-6-0PT forms a Taunton to Castle Cary auto train.
Pursey Short

'County' class No 1001 (Newton Abbot) waits at Taunton platform 1 with an express from the North to Plymouth, 13th June 1946. In the shadows under the canopy, a 'devil' for keeping a water crane frost-free bears a rough notice 'No cups outside' – this was a current ITMA catch-phrase. *Roger Venning*

No 1028 *County of Warwick* (Bristol, Bath Road), only three months old, forming a Taunton to Bristol stopping train at the carriage sidings near Forty Steps Bridge, June 1947. *Roger Venning*

2-6-0 No 6395 (Hereford), making a rare appearance working a freight from Barnstaple, leaves Fairwater yard, February 1947. The approaching railwayman is coming to rebuke the photographer for using a signal as a viewpoint.

Roger Venning

The original two-road Norton Fitzwarren station built by Messrs Phillips of Bristol, opened in 1873 and relieved Taunton of a certain amount of traffic. There was a stone station building on the Up platform, without a sheltering canopy. A timber-built waiting shelter stood on the Down platform. When the line was quadrupled, this layout was replaced by two island platforms with timber buildings; the office block of brick, was separated from the platforms by the Up relief line. The station closed in 1961. The signalmen in the 131-lever box took an extraordinary pride in its cleanliness and insisted on all people working there changing into either slippers or gym shoes. The goods yard handled train-loads of apples from local orchards. It closed on 6th July 1964, but on 27th February 1983 the former Up relief line, latterly the access to the Minehead branch, became the Taunton Cider Company's private siding, the first traffic from it being forwarded on 1st March 1983. At present a limited number of special trains are granted access to the preserved West Somerset Railway via this siding.

About a mile to the west was Victory Siding, chiefly used for loading sugar beet and for shunting off any wagon which had developed a hot box. In 1943, the Down relief road was extended west of Norton Fitzwarren as far as Victory Siding to form a Down loop, the former siding being incorporated and a replacement siding laid. This new loop was long enough to hold three goods trains, each of 60 wagons, standing head-to-tail.

Almost three miles beyond was Poole Siding laid in 1893 to serve William Thomas & Co Ltd's brick and tile works. The firm had a system of two-foot gauge tramways worked by internal combustion locomotives. The firm's line ceased operation in 1967, but Poole Siding itself closed in 1959.

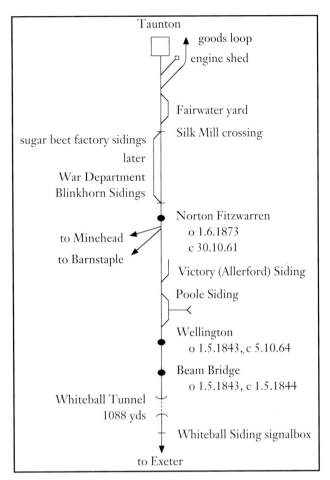

Diagrammatic map of the route from Taunton to Whiteball Siding

No 5998 *Trevor Hall* (Plymouth, Laira) passes Norton Fitzwarren with a Birkenhead to Kingswear and Penzance express on 6th April 1950. The train will be divided at Exeter.
Pursey Short

Norton Fitzwarren, view Down, c.1903, well before the track was quadrupled.

An Exeter to Taunton stopping train, hauled by No 6811 *Cranbourne Grange* (Cardiff), leaves Norton Fitzwarren on 6th April 1950.
Pursey Short

2-6-0 No 7314 (Taunton) heads a Taunton to Barnstaple train away from Norton Fitzwarren in September 1946. Notice the token exchanger on the tender; also the mass of point rodding at the foot of the photograph.
Roger Venning

A 'Bulldog', believed to be No 3443 *Chaffinch*, enters Norton Fitzwarren, c.1937, on the Up relief line, the two porters having crossed ready to assist passengers. The station office building, unusually detached from a platform, is to the right of the locomotive. The Minehead branch curves off to the right.

Lens of Sutton

2-6-0 No 7337 works the 2.24pm Barnstaple to Taunton on 30th May 1964.

R A Lumber

An Up broad gauge express passing Norton Fitzwarren Junction, c.1891. Note the mixed gauge track. *Author's Collection*

No 3819 (Banbury) passes Victory Siding with a Down freight, 28th March 1948. The hedge to the left forms an unusual Great Western boundary, post and wire being more common.
Pursey Short

Looking uncared for, London, Midland & Scottish Railway Class 8F No 8406 (Didcot), built by the GWR at Swindon, waits in Victory Siding with a Down goods for Plymouth, 6th July 1946. *Roger Venning*

No 4337 (Birkenhead) waits at Victory Siding for clear signals before proceeding light engine to Exeter, 8th July 1946. Notice the water tower. *Roger Venning*

The 9.30am Plymouth to Paddington express, hauled by No 5019 *Treago Castle* (Bristol, Bath Road), passes Victory Siding signalbox. Although taken on 28th March 1948, less than three months after Nationalisation, the tender is already lettered 'British Railways' in GWR-style characters. The first two coaches are ex-LMS stock. The corrugated iron hut, right, is an oil store for signal lamp fuel.

Pursey Short

The line from Bridgwater through Taunton to Norton Fitzwarren is either level, or nearly so, but beyond Norton Fitzwarren rises to cross the edge of the Blackdown Hills at Whiteball Summit. The gradient of 1 in 369 up from Norton Fitzwarren steepens west of Victory Siding for about a mile at 1 in 203, and a mile at 1 in 174 before Poole Siding.

Wellington, originally a simple two-road station, was re-modelled in 1931–2, with the platforms moved outwards to be served by loop roads, thus enabling through trains to overtake on new centre roads. Following the closure of the station in 1964, the Up platform road was taken out of use on 23rd May 1965, while the former Down platform road has more recently become an engineer's siding. Only one water crane was ever provided, and this was sited at the west end of the Up platform and intended only for use by banking engines. Water was extracted from a nearby stream, the tank being replenished by an electric pump operated by a float switch.

On Sunday 25th June 1950 a Paignton to Newcastle-upon-Tyne express, composed of ex-London & North Eastern Railway stock, passes under the overbridge east of Wellington station. As No 7907 *Hart Hall* was based at Bristol, St Philip's Marsh, the previous Friday it had probably been hauling freight trains.   *Pursey Short*

The Down 'Cornish Riviera Express' runs through Wellington station, c.1900, hauled by a 4-4-0 and passes a goods train on the Up line.
Author's Collection

On 25th June 1950 a Down express to Kingswear, hauled by a Taunton 'Star' No 4056 *Princess Margaret*, passes on Wellington station's Down through road. Note the quite sharp turn-out beside the goods shed to give access to the Down platform road.

Pursey Short

Hauled by 2-6-0 No 5355 (Pontypool Road), a Down freight passes through Wellington gaining momentum to tackle the bank ahead, 23rd April 1950.

Pursey Short

The original caption to this c.1907 view read: 'Waiting for the Emigration Train. This batch of emigrants, fleeing to better lands, come from the district of Wellington, Somerset, the heart of the English agricultural district.'   *Author's Collection*

'Star' class No 4028 *The Roumanian Monarch* passes with an Up express in 1933. Every one of the ten coaches is different. 'SOM' is added to Wellington's nameboard in case some passengers believe they are in Shropshire.   *Author's Collection*

Beyond the town, the well-known Wellington bank rises steeply for 3¾ miles, chiefly at 1 in 80 to 1 in 90. On weekdays in 1939, there were three Wellington bank engine turns of about eight hours each, while from 6.00am on Sundays to 4.30am on Mondays (a period when there were normally no goods trains), if required, an assistant engine was provided from Taunton instead of Wellington. At the mouth of the 1088-yard long Whiteball Tunnel, the gradient eased to 1 in 127 and at the Devon end, descended past Whiteball Siding signalbox most of the way to Exeter.

Whiteball Siding, off the Down line, provided a refuge for a slow train to be overtaken. Near the signalbox was a crossover for use by returning bank engines, while opposite the box a short engine siding had been added by the 1890s to stable a locomotive for which the signalman had no immediate path. West of the box, a Down relief line, extending to the east end of Burlescombe station, was brought into use on 4th July 1927 but reduced to a train length loop on 26th July 1964. The signalbox, damaged by fire on 28th November 1956, while waiting to be rebuilt, was replaced by a temporary box on the Up side.

An Up express hauled by No 4098 *Kidwelly Castle* (Newton Abbot) leaves Whiteball Tunnel on 19th August 1951. *Pursey Short*

A Down freight, headed by No 7805 *Broome Manor* (Banbury), enters Whiteball Tunnel, 22nd April 1951. *Pursey Short*

The above train is banked by No 4136 (Taunton). More than three years into Nationalisation, its tank sides still bear the initials GWR. In the shadow caused by the exhaust, an old coach body is used as a platelayers' hut. *Pursey Short*

No 3845 (Reading) climbs to Whiteball Tunnel with a through freight on 22nd April 1951. *Pursey Short*

No 4136 (Taunton) banks the above goods train, with No 3845 about to enter Whiteball Tunnel. *Pursey Short*

An inspection train being propelled on the Down line at Whiteball Siding signalbox. The notice reads: 'Catch points are situated 40 yards outside east end of Whiteball Tunnel'.

J F King Collection

Whiteball Siding signalbox: No 2840 (Wrexham, Croes Newydd) passing after a Tilley lamp had ignited much of the box. The sign to the left indicates catch points 2345 yards to the east.

Tony Harvey Collection

3. Taunton to Langport West and Langport East

The story of the line to Langport really started back in the summer of 1844 when the B&ER planned to build a branch to Weymouth from its main line at Durston. It had second thoughts in the autumn and decided to terminate at Yeovil. The contractors Messrs Rigby, completed the line from Yeovil as far as Martock in 1849, but it lay rusting until the remainder to Durston was finished. The delay was caused by a shortage of cash, the company already having heavy financial commitments elsewhere. The contract for the completion of the line was let in 1852 to Messrs Hutchinson & Ritson, while that for the five stations was given to Edward Streeter who had tendered successfully for many B&ER contracts. The single-line branch finally opened to passenger traffic on 1st October 1853 and to goods on 26th October. On 2nd February 1857 trains ran through to the Wilts, Somerset & Weymouth station at Yeovil (Pen Mill).

Friction occurred between the standard and broad gauge factions when in 1867 the standard gauge Somerset & Dorset Railway planned to construct a branch to Bridgwater. This would have been in direct competition with the B&ER, so in order to give standard gauge communication between Yeovil and Bridgwater, as an alternative to the proposed London & South Western and Somerset & Dorset lines, the B&ER was forced to pay £125,000 and lay a third rail from Highbridge, where it made a junction with the Somerset & Dorset lines,

through Bridgwater and Durston to Yeovil. On 30th June 1879 the mixed gauge branch was completely converted to standard gauge and with this change went the nuisance and expense of transhipping goods at Hendford between wagons of the two gauges.

In 1876 the branch became GWR property when the B&ER was amalgamated with the Great Western. To combat road competition the GWR opened unstaffed stations at Thorney & Kingsbury Halt in 1927, and Lyng Halt the following year.

An interesting innovation was a diesel railcar service between Taunton, Yeovil and Weymouth, other stops being made only for staff exchange on the single line sections. The only other through train to Weymouth was the occasional evening excursion which reversed at Yeovil Pen Mill *en route* to the watering place. As its return was after the Yeovil to Durston branch had closed for the night, it travelled via Castle Cary, reversing there. These excursions were generally worked by a Taunton 51XX class 2-6-2T. A regular interesting train was the 4.25pm Taunton to Trowbridge via Yeovil which was 55XX-hauled and proceeded as a through service to Bristol Temple Meads.

The branch closed to passenger traffic on 15th June 1964 and following the opening of Taunton Freight Concentration Depot, goods traffic ceased on 6th July that same year.

'Bulldog' No 3364 *Frank Bibby* (Westbury) heads the 2.33pm Yeovil Pen Mill to Taunton train near Creech St Michael, 12th September 1947.

Pursey Short

Description of the line from Taunton to Langport West

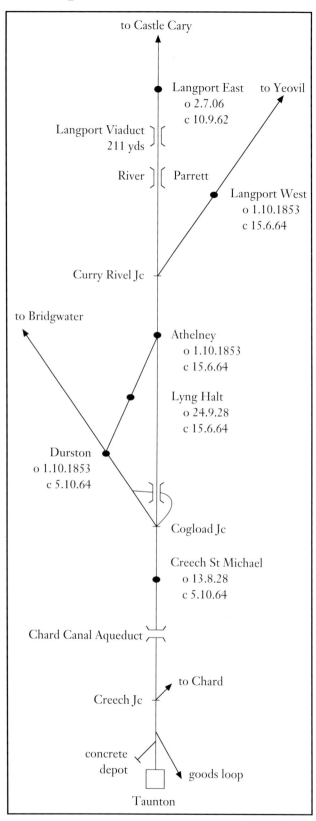

Diagrammatic map of the route from Taunton to Langport

The single-track branch left the Bridgwater line at the north end of Durston station. Lyng Halt, close to the village of East Lyng and about a mile from West Lyng, had a sleeper-built platform face and edging, and a timber waiting shelter. The branch joined the double-track main line from Cogload Junction west of Athelney station and immediately east of the Up and Down passing loop opened in October 1943 to ease wartime traffic congestion by giving faster trains an opportunity to overtake a slower, or one of lesser importance. Athelney station had timber buildings, one of which was purchased by the local cricket club after closure for use as a pavilion.

The line passed through a low-lying area subject to flooding, one of the earliest instances being on the afternoon of Wednesday 20th November 1875 when the first of an Up train was put out by the floodwater which came within three inches of the coach floor. The line was covered up to 3 ft 4 ins deep for one and a half miles. The consternation of passengers stranded in the flood and dreading it growing deeper while awaiting rescue by pilot engine, can be imagined. The *Taunton Courier* reported: 'When the wind was rough, waves beat against the carriages'.

When the line was doubled, the section from Athelney to Curry Rivel Junction was raised above flood level and frequent openings made to allow water to run away. Near Oath, the Stathe to Curry Rivel lane is carried over the railway by a six-span girder bridge, odd in appearance due to the fact that five of the spans are of different pattern.

At Curry Rivel Junction the Langport West line curved southwards. When the Curry Rivel Junction to Castle Cary line was built, the section from Curry Rivel Junction to Langport West was doubled on 2nd July 1906 in order that a train proceeding towards Taunton and waiting to join the main line at Curry Rivel Junction would not block a Taunton to Langport West train. This alteration involved replacing the signalbox on the Up platform with a new one sited at the end of the Down. Langport West had a Brunel-type stone building, the almost flat awning extending all round the structure. A private siding led to Messrs Mead & Sons lime works. 'West' was added to its name on 2nd July 1906 when Langport East was opened on the Curry Rivel Junction to Castle Cary line.

On summer Saturdays, two afternoon trains from Taunton to Yeovil via Durston had scheduled waits of ten minutes at Athelney in order to allow an Up express to pass, while a couple of Up branch trains were not allowed on the busy main line at all and, when they had reached Langport West, returned to Yeovil. Passengers for Taunton had to continue their journey by bus. Later a path was found for a Taunton to Yeovil train, but to avoid delaying expresses, it ran to Langport West non-stop there to wait half-an-hour before proceeding to its destination.

Down Trains. YEOVIL BRANCH. Week Days.

Single Line Yeovil (Pen Mill) to Langport West, worked by Electric Train Staff or Token. Crossing Station is Martock.

M.P. Mileage from Paddington. M.	C.	STATIONS.	Ruling Gradient.	Time allowance for Ordinary Freight Trains (See page 2) Point to Point Times	Allow for Stop.	Allow for Start.	B Passenger. arr.	dep.	K Freight. arr.	dep.	B Passenger. arr.	dep.	B Diesel dep.	B Passenger. SUSPENDED arr.	dep.	B Passenger. SO arr.	dep.	K Bridgwater Freight. SX arr.	dep.	K Bridgwater Freight. SO arr.	dep.	S.R. Pass. dep.
				Mins.	Mins.	Mins.	a.m.	a.m.	a.m.	a.m.	a.m.	a.m.	a.m.	a.m.	a.m.	p.m.	p.m.	p.m.	p.m.	p.m.	p.m.	p.m.
141	27 W	**YEOVIL P.M.**	113 F.	—	—	2	—	7 8	—	9 40	—	9 57	10 45	—	11 43	—	12 46	—	1 0	—	1 0	1 15
141	73 W	Yeovil Town	215 R.	1	1	1	7 10	7 13	9 45	9 49	9 59	10 1	10 17	11 45	11 47	12 49	12 51	C	S	C	S	1 17
142	72 W	Hendford Halt ←■	150 R.	3	1	2	—	7 16	9 54	•10 13	—	10 4		—	11 50	—	12 54	1 8	•1 20	1 8X	•1 47	
146	40 W	Montacute	85 R.	10	2	1	7 24	7 25	C	R	10 12	10 12½		11 58	11 59	1 2	1 3	1 32	•1 48	2 2	2 15	
149	14 W	Martock	106 R.	8	2	1	7 31	X7 40	10 31	•12 27	10 17½	10 18		12 4	X12 5	1 8	1 9	1 58	•3 45	2 25	•3 45	
151	73 W	Thorney and K. Halt	123 F.	—	—	—	7 45	7 46	1234C	R1248	10 24	10 25		12 10	12 11	1 14	1 15	3 51	3 58	3 51	3 58	
154	22 W	Langport West	83 F.	12	1	1	7 51	7 53	12 55	—	10 29	X10 32		12 15	12 16	1 19	—	4 3	4 21	4 3	4 21	
130	77 Z	Curry Rivel Jct.	264 F.	2	1	1	7	54			10	34		12	17			C 4	23 R	C 4	23 R	
134	71 Z	Athelney	284 F.	10V	1	1	8 1	8 2	RR to Curry Rivel Jct.		10 41	10 42		12 21	12 25			4 35	•5 32	4 35	•5 32	
159	65 W	Lyng Halt	330 R.	—	—	—	8 4	8 5					RL	12 26½	12 27			—	—	—	—	
157	29 ‡	Durston	256 R.	6	1	1	8 9	8 12						12 30½	12 32			5 40	•6 55	5 40	•6 55	
158	31 ‡	Cogload	330 R.	—	—	—	R	L			M	L		R	L							
160	25 ‡	Creech St. M. Halt	288 R.	—	—	—	8 17	8 18			—	—		—	—							
160	57 ‡	Creech Junction	L.	9V	1	1	R	L			M	L		R	L							
162	63 ‡	Taunton East Jct.	200 R.	—	—	—	R	L			M	L §		R	L							
163	11 ‡	**TAUNTON**	221 R.	6	1	—	8 23	—			10 53	—		12 42	—							

§—Runs on Sats.

STATIONS.	B Passenger. arr.	dep.	G Engine. arr.	dep.	B Passenger. arr.	dep.	S.R. Pass. dep.	B Passenger. arr.	dep.	K Freight. arr.	dep.	B Passenger. arr.	dep.	Sundays. D Milk Empties. arr.	dep.	D Engine and Van. arr.	dep.	B Castle Cary Auto. arr.	dep.
	p.m.	p.m.	p.m.	p.m.	p.m.	p.m.	p.m.	p.m.	p.m.	p.m.	p.m.	p.m.	p.m.	p.m.	p.m.	p.m.	p.m.	p.m.	p.m.
YEOVIL P.M.	—	2 33	—	3‖20	—	4 0	4 44		5 52	—	6 5	—	7 45	—	1†20				
Yeovil Town	2 35	2 38	C	S	4 2	4 9	4 46	5 54	6 0	C	S	7 47	8 2	1†22	1†32	—	4† 0		
Hendford Halt ←■	—	2 41	C	S	—	4 12		—	6 3	6 12	•6 55	—	8 5	C	S	C	S		
Montacute	2 49	2 50	—	—	4 20	4 21		6 11	6 12	—	—	8 13	8 14	—	—	—	—		
Martock	2 55	X2 56	3‖40	X —	4 26	X4 27		6 17	6 18	7 13	•7 35	8 19	8 20	1†44	1†45	C	S		
Thorney and K. Halt	3 1	3 2			4 32	4 33		6 23	6 24	C	R	8 25	8 26	1†50	—	4†17	—		
Langport West	3 6	3 7			4 37	4 39		6 28	X6 29	7 47	•8 15	8 30	8 31					—	3 25
Curry Rivel Jct.	3	8			4	40		6	30	8	17	8	32					3 27	3 32
Athelney	3 15	3 17			4 47	4 48		6 37	6 38	8 27	•8 52	8 39	8 40						
Lyng Halt	3 19	3 20			4 49½	4 50½		6 39½	6 40	—	—	8 42	8 43						
Durston	3 24	3 27			4 54	X4 55		6 43½	6 46	9 0	—	8 46½	8 48						
Cogload	R	L			R	L		R	L			R	L						
Creech St. M. Halt	3 32	3 34			5 0	5 1		6 51	6 52			8 53	8 54						
Creech Junction	R	L			M	L		R	L			M	L						
Taunton East Jct.	M	L			M	L		M	L			M	L						
TAUNTON	3 40	K			5 7	Q		6 57	—			9 0	—						

K—Advertised to arrive Taunton 3 42 p.m.
V—14 minutes, Athelney to Creech Junction.
W—Via Chippenham and Yeovil. Z—Via Lavington and Somerton.
‡—Via Box and Bristol (T.M.)

Q—Advertised to arrive Taunton 5.10 p.m.

Up Trains. YEOVIL BRANCH—continued. Week Days.

Distance. M.	C.	STATIONS.	Ruling Gradient.	Time allowance for Freight Trains (See page 2.) Point to Point times.	Allow for Stop.	Allow for Start.	K Freight. arr.	dep.	B Passenger.¹ arr.	dep.	B Diesel dep.	B Passenger. arr.	dep.	B Passenger. SUSPENDED arr.	dep.	S.R. Pass. dep.	B Passenger. SO arr.	dep.	B Passenger. arr.	dep.	S.R. Pass. dep.	K Freight. arr.	dep.
				Mins.	Mins.	Mins.	a.m.	a.m.	a.m.	a.m.	a.m.	a.m.	a.m.	a.m.	a.m.	p.m.	p.m.	p.m.	p.m.	p.m.	p.m.	p.m.	p.m.
—	—	**TAUNTON**	—	—	—	1	—	5 40	—	6 52		—	9 55	—	11 30				—	2 5			
0	28	Taunton East Jct.	200 F.	—	—	—	R	L	R	L		R	L	M	L				R	L			
2	35	Creech Junction	221 F.	6	1	1	R 5	40 L	R	L		R	L	M 11	35 L				R	L			
2	66	Creech St. M. Halt	L.	—	—	—	—	—	6 57	6 58		10 0	10 1	—	—				2 10	2 12			
4	60	Cogload	288 F.	—	—	—	—	—	—	—		—	—	—	—				—	—			
5	62	Durston	330 F.	9	1	1	5 55	•7 15	7 3	7 5		10 6	10 9						2 17	2 19			
7	34	Lyng Halt	330 F.	—	—	—	—	—	7 8½	7 9		10 13	10 14						2 23	2 24			
7	78 §	Athelney	330 F.	6	1	1	7 23	•7 38	7 11	7 12		10 16	10 17	11 42	11 43				2 26	2 29			
11	75 §	Curry Rivel Jct.	264 R.	10	1	1	C 7	50 R	7	19		10	24	11	50				2	36			
12	56 §	Langport West	264 F.	2	1	1	7 52	8 15	7 20	7 22		10 26	X10 31	11 51	11 52		—	1 37	2 38	2 40		—	3 15
15	0 §	Thorney and K. Halt	83 R.	—	—	—	C	R	7 26	7 27		10 35	10 36	11 56	11 57		1 42	1 43	2 44	2 45		3 22C	R3 32
17	64 §	Martock	123 R.	13	1	2	8 30	•9 0	7 32	X7 35		10 41	10 42	12 2	X12 6		1 43	1 49	2 51	X2 57		3 40	•4 30
20	38 §	Montacute	106 F.	10	1	2	9 12	•9 22	7 40	7 41		10 47	10 48	12 11	12 12		1 54	1 55	3 2	3 3		4 38	•4 42
24	6 §	Hendford Halt ←■	85 F.	10	2	1	9 35	•10 38	—	7 49		—	10 56	—	12 20		—	2 3	—	3 11		4 57	•5 7
25	5 §	Yeovil Town	150 F.	3	1	1	C	S	7 51	7 55	10 50	10 58	11 0	12 22	12 25	12 55	2 5	2 8	3 13	3 16	4 25	C	S
25	51 §	**YEOVIL P.M.**	215 F.	1	1	—	10 44	—	7 57	—	10 52	11 3	—	12 27	—	12 57	2 10	—	3 18	X —	4 27	5 13	—

S.R. Pass.: 5 mins. later on Saturdays.

§—Distance via Durston and Lyng, 21 chains extra.

STATIONS.	C Milk. arr.	dep.	B Trowbridge Passenger. arr.	dep.	B Passenger. arr.	dep.	B Passenger. arr.	dep.	K Freight. arr.	dep.	Sundays. B 11.45 a.m. Westbury Auto. arr.	dep.	C Milk. arr.	dep.	C Milk. arr.	dep.
	p.m.	p.m.	p.m.	p.m.	p.m.	p.m.	p.m.	p.m.	p.m.	p.m.	p.m.	p.m.	p.m.	p.m.	p.m.	p.m.
TAUNTON			—	4 40	—	5 52	—	8 20								
Taunton East Jct.			R	L	R	L	R	L								
Creech Junction			R	L	R	L	R	L								
Creech St. M. Halt			4 45	4 46	5 57	5 58	8 25	8 26								
Cogload			—	—	—	—	—	—								
Durston			4 51	X4 56	6 3	6 8	8 31	8 32	—	10 15						
Lyng Halt			4 59½	5 0	6 12	6 13	8 35½	8 36	—	—						
Athelney			5 2	5 3	6 15	6 17	8 37½	8 38½	C 10	22 S						
Curry Rivel Jct.			5	10	6	24	8	46½	10	32	1†37	1†41				
Langport West			5 11	5 14	6 25	X6 29	8 46½	8 49	10 35	10 40	1†43	—				
Thorney and K. Halt			5 18	5 19	6 33	6 34	8 53	8 54	—	—			—	3 30	—	5 0
Martock	—	5 5	5 24	5 26	6 39	6 40	8 58	9 1	10 55	11 15			C	S	5 5	5 10
Montacute	—	—	5 31	5 32	6 45	6 46	9 6	9 7	—	—			—	—	—	—
Hendford Halt ←■	C	S	5 39	5 40	—	6 51	—	9 15	11 38	11 50			C	S	C	S
Yeovil Town	5 21	5 29	5 42	5 48	6 56	6 58	9 17	9 23	11 55L	12 0			3 45	—	5 22	5 38
YEOVIL P.M.	5 31	—	5 50	X6 0	7 0	—	9 25	—	12 5	—					5 40	—

Extract from the GWR working timetable for summer 1947

Athelney, view Down, 21st August 1962. After closure, one of these platform buildings was purchased by the local cricket club for use as a pavilion.

Author

Lyng Halt, view Down, c.1962. Notice the fire bucket hanging on the corner of the timber waiting shelter. *Lens of Sutton*

Langport West, view Up, after 17th April 1906 when the new signalbox was opened. Note the sheeted wagons in the goods yard, left. On the wide platform stands a trolley well-laden with crates. *Author's Collection*

A Taunton to Castle Cary auto train, headed by No 5406 (Frome), in Forty Steps Siding before entering Taunton station, 17th December 1946.
Roger Venning

The Langport East Line

Towards the end of the 19th century, critics of the GWR claimed that the company's initials stood for 'Great Way Round'. To a certain extent this was true and the GWR, realising it, decided to shorten the route to the West. The new way from Reading to Taunton via Westbury and Castle Cary used existing lines for part of the way, though their alignment was improved to main line standards, but between Castle Cary and Curry Rivel Junction, (and also from Patney & Chirton to Westbury), a completely new track had to be built. For the four miles from Curry Rivel Junction to Athelney, the new line followed the Yeovil branch which was raised above flood level and doubled. An entirely new line was built from Athelney to Cogload Junction, by-passing Lyng Halt and Durston Junction. This explains why the single track to Lyng Halt existed – until one knows its history, it seemed quite superfluous.

The new line to Langport East, Somerton and Castle Cary was built by Messrs Wills of Manchester and opened to goods trains on 2nd April 1906. It was the usual practice for goods trains to use a new railway before passenger trains ran over a line, in order that embankments could be compacted and any settling adjusted.

Through goods trains to the West used the new line from 11th June 1906. It had been planned that express passenger trains would first use the line on 2nd July, but on the first of that month, a portion of Box Tunnel caved in. West of England expresses were diverted via Castle Cary a day earlier than planned. As it happened, this new line was the only route available to the West on 1st July, for the London & South Western line was blocked at Salisbury by a tragic crash caused by the Up boat express from Plymouth travelling at too great a speed round a sharp curve. In 1962 the stations between Athelney and Castle Cary were closed to passenger traffic. They had never really justified themselves, as the line was mainly intended to be used as a through route.

From Curry Rivel Junction the main line rises for a mile at 1 in 264, crossing the River Parrett by a viaduct of two blue brick and three steel spans, that over the river itself being of 105-ft span. A little further east is Langport Viaduct of 10 blue brick arches, whose foundations were sunk 50 ft to below the peat and bog. Langport East was a typical red-brick station of the period, conifers planted by the railway mellowing the earthworks.

Hand-operated cranes lowering a girder to replace a brick arch on Langport Viaduct. The span of the bridge over the River Parrett is on the far right.

J F King Collection

BR Standard Class 3MT 2-6-2T No 82044 with the 5.00pm Taunton to Castle Cary train, at Langport East, 21st August 1962.

Author.

4. Taunton to Thornfalcon

The story of the Taunton to Chard line started back in 1830 when some enterprising local people invited an Exeter engineer, James Green, to make a report on the feasibility of building a canal linking Chard with the Bridgwater & Taunton Canal. Green carried out the survey, but suggested that a railway would be more in keeping with the times and a better business proposition. However his employers thought that they knew best and a canal was built three years later. During the Railway Mania of 1845 when so many wildcat schemes were put forward, Chard was mentioned in two plans for a rail link between the Bristol and English Channels. Such a scheme would naturally have taken traffic from the Bridgwater & Taunton and the Chard canals, so the owners of these waterways countered this suggestion with a railway of their own. Parliament refused to grant permission for a line, but sanctioned a railway from Creech to Ilminster. The Chard Canal Company immediately applied to Parliament to convert its waterway from Ilminster to Chard into a railway, the Act being duly passed the following year, 1847. The Chard Canal Company changed its name to the Chard Railway Company but the only railway part of it was the title, for the concern was heavily in debt and had no funds to build a line. The local people, quite undaunted, revived the proposal in 1852. An Act was passed the following year to convert the canal and extend the line to Taunton. Because of a lack of capital, this line also came to naught.

In 1863 a short branch was opened from the London & South Western Railway's main line, to Chard, and although this brief line gave them some satisfaction, the people of Chard still looked towards a link with their county town. The answer was the Chard & Taunton Railway Act of 1861 which gave both the B&ER and the LSWR powers of subscription. The former were about the only investors, local people not wishing to chance their money, so a further Act came before Parliament the following year, permitting the B&ER to increase its subscription. Even this proved insufficient, so in 1863 the B&ER was granted an Act allowing it to take over the powers of the Chard & Taunton Company and build a broad gauge line.

Lady Anna Gore Langton performed the ceremony of cutting the first sod early in September 1863. Logan & Rennie were the contractors, the engineer being a local man, John Fox of Hatch. All engineering works, including the 154-yd long Hatch Tunnel, were built wide enough to accommodate double track, though only one was ever laid. Unlike most of the B&ER, points were operated by levers rather than capstans. The *Somerset County Gazette* for 16th September 1865 reported a delay in opening the line until the spring of the following year. Eventually, on 25th August 1866, it carried the following article:

The Taunton–Chard Railway

We understand there is every probability of this line being opened very shortly for traffic. It is expected the formal opening is to take place in the early part of September. The stations on the line are not yet fitted up, and the signals have also to be completed. The line itself, however, is fit for traffic, as was shown on Tuesday last, when the directors of the Bristol and Exeter Railway ran a train from this town to Ilminster in order to convey the archaeologists thither. The train was accompanied by Mr Blackmore, and the distance from here to Ilminster was accomplished in half an hour, including a stoppage to take on a truck from the down line. There is but one tunnel, but there are several deep cuttings. As the traveller emerges from these there are a number of pretty bits of scenery cropping up, and glimpses obtained of many a homestead which the occupants rushed out to see the novel sight of a passenger train in their neighbourhood.

At Ilminster a large number of persons had assembled to witness the arrival of the train, and a good deal of interest was manifested in this precursor of increased traffic, and, no doubt of increased prosperity to the town.

On the return of the train in the evening there was a large assemblage of persons, and some hearty cheers were set up as it moved off. The return journey occupied scarcely so long as that in the morning, although, there being no lights, it was necessary to proceed with caution.

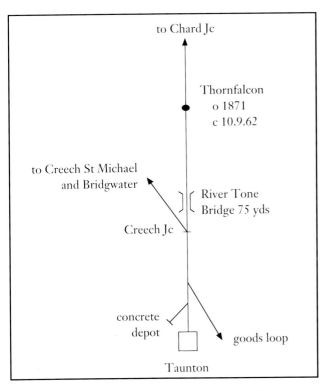

Diagrammatic map of the route from Taunton to Thornfalcon

CHARD BRANCH.

Single Line worked by Electric Train Staff between Creech Junction and Hatch, and Hatch and Ilminster, during the time Hatch Box is open; when closed, worked by Electric Token, between Creech Junction and Ilminster; Electric Train Staff between Ilminster and Chard. Train Staff between Chard and Chard Junction, in accordance with the "Regulations for Working Single Lines by one engine in steam or two or more engines coupled together."

The Crossing Stations are Creech Junction and Chard.

When absolutely necessary two Freight Trains, or a Passenger and a Freight Train, may cross at Hatch or Ilminster, on the understanding that the Passenger Train is always kept on the Running Line, and that if the Passenger Train has to stop at Hatch or Ilminster it must stop at the Platform.

DOWN TRAINS. — WEEK DAYS.

Distance from Chard.	STATIONS.	Ruling Gradient.	Point-to-Point Times.	Allow for Stop.	Allow for Start.	K Freight. arr.	K Freight. dep.	B Passenger. arr.	B Passenger. dep.	G Engine and Van. dep.	K Freight. arr.	K Freight. dep.	B Mixed. dep.	G Engine and Van. arr.	G Engine and Van. dep.	B Passenger. arr.	B Passenger. dep.	K Frght dep.	B Mixed. RR dep.
M. C.			Mins.	Mins.	Mins.	a.m.	a.m.	a.m.	a.m.	a.m.	a.m.	a.m.	a.m.	a.m.	a.m.	p.m.	p.m.	noon.	p.m.
— —	Chard Junction (SR)	—	—				7 40		8 28										
— —	Chard Town (S.R.)	—	—							9 22		10 56			11 32				1 10
— —	CHARD	—			1	7 50	8 0	8 37	x9 15	9 24		10 15	11 6	11 34			12 0		1 20
3 20	Donyatt Halt	77 F.			1	8 2		9 21	9 22						RR	12 6	12 7		
3 78	Ilminster	141 F.	9	1	1			9 25	9 26		10 25	12 45			Frght Sats.	12 10	12 11		
5 25	Ilton Halt	100 F.						9 29	9 30							12 14	12 15		
8 51	Hatch	125 F.	11	1	1			9 36	9 37		12 56	1 10				12 21	12 22		
11 49	Thornfalcon	80 F.	7	2	1			9 43	9 44		C R					12 28	12 29		A
12 53	Creech Sidings	97 F.									1 23	1 30						1 5	
12 61	Creech Junction	288 R.	—					C9 46 S		C13 35 S						C12 31 S		C S	
15 16	TAUNTON		9	1				9 51		1 40						12 36		1 11	

DOWN TRAINS. — WEEK DAYS — continued.

STATIONS.	B Passenger. arr.	B Passenger. dep.	G Engine and Van. RR SO dep.	G Engine and Van. RR SO dep.	B Pass SO dep.	K Frght SX dep.	K Freight. arr.	K Freight. dep.	B Passenger. arr.	B Passenger. dep.	B Pass. dep.	G Engine SX dep.	B Pass. dep.	B Passenger. arr.	B Passenger. dep.
	p.m.	p.m.	p.m.	p.m.	p.m.	p.m.	p.m.	p.m.	p.m.	p.m.	p.m.	p.m.	p.m.	p.m.	p.m.
Chard Junction (S.R.)			1 53	2 15	3 5					4 55	5 50	6 20	7 7		
Chard Town (S.R.)		1 30	x 1 55	2 25		4 0					5 59	6 30	x 7 16		
CHARD	1 36	1 37		x 3 14		4 3		4 15	5 4	x5 15					7 45
Donyatt Halt	1 40	1 43							5 21	5 22				7 51	7 51
Ilminster	1 46	1 47					4 25	x 5 5	5 25	5 27				7 54	7 57
Ilton Halt	1 54	1 56							5 30	5 31				8 0	8 01
Hatch	2 2	2 3					5 15	5 20	5 37	5 38				8 6	8 8
Thornfalcon									5 44	5 45				8 14	8 15
Creech Siding															
Creech Junction	C2 13 S						C5 28 S		C5 47 S					C8 17 S	
TAUNTON	2 10						5 35		5 52					8 22	

§—May be run as a Mixed Train between Chard Junction and Chard when required for cattle traffic only.   x—1 minute later on Saturdays.

CHARD BRANCH—continued.

UP TRAINS. — WEEK DAYS.

M.P. Mileage.	STATIONS.	Ruling Gradient.	Point-to-Point Times.	Allow for Stop.	Allow for Start.	B Passenger. arr.	B Passenger. dep.	K Freight. arr.	K Freight. dep.	K Freight. arr.	K Freight. dep.	B Passenger. dep.	K Frght dep.	B Passenger. dep.	K Frght dep.	B Passenger. dep.	K Frght dep.	B Passenger. dep.	K Freight. SO arr.	K Freight. SO dep.	K Frght SO RR dep.	B Passenger. SO dep.
M. C.			Mins.	Mins.	Mins.	a.m.	a.m.	a.m.	a.m.	a.m.	a.m.	a.m.	a.m.	a.m.	a.m.	a.m.	a.m.	p.m.	a.m.	a.m.	p.m.	p.m.
0 0	TAUNTON	—	—		1		5 30				6 45			8 30			11 5				11 30		
0 11	Creech Junction	—	—			C3 34 S				C4 52 S				C8 44 S			C11 58 S				C11 37 S		
1 15	Creech Sidings	—	—																				
4 13	Thornfalcon	97 R.	9	1	2									8 37			11 10		11 40	11 50			
7 39	Hatch	80 R.	8	1	1					CR	ST			8 45			11 20		12 0	12 23			
8 66	Ilton Halt	125 R.													8 53			11 28					
9 44	Ilminster	141 R.	11	1	1	5 53	5 59			7 15	7 18			8 59			11 34		12 35	1 5			
12 64	CHARD	77 R.	11			6 10		7 7	7 5	8 0		8 10	9 5	x9 10	9 34	11 18	11 45	12 10	1 18		1 30	2 0	
— —	Chard Town (S.R.)	—	—					7 7	7 17			9 7		11 20							1 32		
— —	Chard Jct. (S.R.)	—	—					7 23		8 18		9 42		12 18								2 8	

UP TRAINS. — WEEK DAYS — continued.

Mileage from Taunton.	STATIONS.	K Freight. SX arr.	K Freight. SX dep.	K Frght RR dep.	B Frght RR SO dep.	B Passenger. arr.	B Passenger. dep.	B Passenger. dep.	B Passenger. arr.	B Passenger. dep.	B Pass. dep.	B Passenger. dep.	K Freight. SX arr.	K Freight. SX dep.	B Passenger. arr.	B Passenger. dep.
M. C.		a.m.	a.m.	p.m.	p.m.	p.m.	p.m.	p.m.	p.m.	p.m.	p.m.	p.m.	p.m.	p.m.	p.m.	p.m.
0 0	TAUNTON		11 45	12 30			2 35			4 32							6 45
2 32	Creech Junction	C11 51 S		C S	12 38				C4 36 S								C6 49 S
2 43	Creech Sidings	11 53	12 0														
3 47	Thornfalcon	12 4	12 10			2 42	2 44			4 38	4 39					6 51	6 52
6 43	Hatch	12 20	1 0			2 51	2 53			4 46	4 47					6 59	7 0
9 71	Ilton Halt					3 0	3 1			4 51	4 53					7 7	7 8
11 18	Ilminster	1 11	1 59			3 4	3 9			4 58	5 1					7 11	7 14
11 76	Donyatt Halt					3 12	3 13			5 4	5 5					7 17	7 18
15 16	CHARD	2 10	2 39			3 20 x	—		4 20	5 12	x —	5 36		6 4		7 25 x	
15 43	Chard Town (S.R.)	2 33		2 40					4 28			5 44		6 12	6 53		
19 44	Chard Jct. (S.R.)			2 50										6 43			

Extract from the GWR working timetable for summer 1947

70

CHARD BRANCH—continued.

DOWN TRAINS. — WEEK DAYS—continued.

STATIONS.	A — Passenger and Mail.		B — Passenger. SO																			
	arr.	dep.	arr.	dep.																		
	p.m.	p.m.	p.m.	p.m.																		
Chard Junction (S.R.)	—	9 10	—	9 5J																		
Chard Town (S.R.)																						
CHARD	9 19	x9 40	9 53	10 0																		
Donyatt Halt			10 6	10 7																		
Ilminster	9 48	9 51	10 10	10 11																		
Ilton Halt			10 14	10 15																		
Hatch	—	—	10 21	10 22																		
Thornfalcon	—	—	10 28	10 29																		
Creech Siding																						
Creech Junction	C10	◦S	C10	◦◦S																		
TAUNTON	10 10		10 36	—																		

UP TRAINS. — WEEK DAYS—continued.

STATIONS.	B — Pass.	B — Passenger SO																				
	dep	arr.	dep.																			
	p.m.	p.m.	p.m.																			
TAUNTON		—	8 55																			
Creech Junction		C³	8⁹S																			
Creech Siding																						
Thornfalcon		9 1	9 2																			
Hatch		9 7	9 8																			
Ilton Halt		9 15	9 16																			
Ilminster		9 19	9 20																			
Donyatt Halt		9 23	9 24																			
CHARD	8 43	9 31	x9 32																			
Chard Town (S.R.)	—		—																			
Chard Junction (S.R.)	8 51	9 40	—																			

The line was opened, without ceremony, to passenger traffic on 11th September, but as was the case on many local branch lines, the goods sheds were incomplete and freight could not be carried until the following March. The *Somerset County Gazette* of 15th September 1866 carried the report:

> There are stations at Hatch and Ilminster which are built of brick with freestone facings, and have somewhat pretty appearance. There is but one tunnel near Hatch, but there are several deep cuttings through layers of rock. The masonry of the bridges, of which there are several, appears to be of a substantial character. The first train left Chard at half past seven o'clock on Tuesday morning, and was accompanied by Mr Dyke and Mr Blackmore, performing the journey punctually in the time of forty minutes. A tolerably large number of passengers came by train, and throughout the day the traffic was larger than expected. It is intended for the present to run five trains to and from on week days and two on Sundays. If a temporary platform were erected at Creech, and one train each way were to stop there on market days, it would be a boon to farmers in the neighbourhood; and the increased traffic, we are inclined to think would quite pay for the slight increase in expenditure or trouble it might occasion.

The contractors were required to maintain the line for 12 months after completion and a man whose job it was to pack ballast under the sleepers was run over and killed just south of Creech Junction. It was not known whether he committed suicide or was asleep.

When in 1878 the B&ER decided to convert its branches to standard gauge, it purposely kept the Chard branch broad for as long as possible in order to prevent the standard gauge London & South Western Railway from obtaining running powers over the line as far as Taunton. However, when the decision finally to abolish the broad gauge was taken, the branch was the first of the last group of lines to be converted. This was carried out on Sunday 19th July 1891, the 13-mile long branch being changed to standard gauge in only 20 hours. The line had great possibilities of being developed as a through route between the Midlands and the holiday towns of Seaton, Lyme Regis and Sidmouth, but this chance was never seized. Passenger trains were insufficiently used, so the service was withdrawn from 10th September 1962, the goods trains succumbing two years later on 6th July 1964.

During World War Two the Taunton Stop Line was constructed from the Parrett Estuary to Seaton. It consisted of 355 pill boxes, so that had the Germans invaded the South Western peninsula, they could have been contained and not allowed to spread to the rest of the country. This defence line followed the Chard branch. The pill boxes were concealed – the one at Ilton was like a water tank, and that at Ilminster, a signalbox. This camouflage was designed by Oliver Messel, a theatrical film designer.

Chard branch trains caused a problem to out-of-course main line traffic, as leaving Taunton they had to cross all the running lines and then had to cross back again at Creech Junction.

The Chard branch curved away from the main line at Creech Junction, almost three and a half miles east of Taunton station and just before Creech St Michael Halt. Set in the angle between the main and branch lines was Creech paper mill. Inwards traffic was made up of coal from local mines at Coalpit Heath and from Radstock, this traffic ending in the early sixties. Outwards traffic consisted of vans loaded with small consignments which were taken to Taunton and off-loaded into other vans for transport elsewhere. Outwards traffic finished about 1949. Just beyond the junction, the branch crossed the River Tone by a five-span bridge.

Thornfalcon had a timber platform and waiting shelter. Latterly the platform was renewed in concrete, the timber surface becoming slippery in wet weather. Unusually the main passenger approach to the station was across a goods siding, latterly very busy with waste paper and coal traffic. Originally Thorne Falcon, the station was re-named Thorne in July 1890 and Thornfalcon on 1st January 1902.

Building an overbridge near Thorn Falcon, c.1865.

Edward Jeboult Collection

Thornfalcon station, view towards Creech Junction, pre-1912. Notice the timber platform and buildings. The track is on longitudinal sleepers.

Lens of Sutton

Thornfalcon from the north, 21st August 1962.

Author

No 5543 (Taunton) waits to leave platform 2 with a Taunton to Chard train on 1st June 1946. The first vehicle, a corridor coach, in the wartime all-brown livery; the 'B' set is painted chocolate and cream.

Roger Vennir

No 9718 (Taunton) on a branch goods train to Chard in early 1947. It is standing in the goods loop at Obridge waiting to join the main line. The light-coloured building to the right of the locomotive buffer housed locomotive No 24 which shunted in the concrete yard.

Roger Vennin

5. Taunton to Milverton

The North Devon Railway reached Barnstaple from Exeter in 1854, but a glance at a map shows that a more direct route to the town was by a route proceeding due westwards from Taunton. The Devon & Somerset Railway Act was passed in 1864 and although its planned extension to Ilfracombe was rejected, the company received powers for building a connecting line at Barnstaple and being the joint owner of a mixed gauge route to Ilfracombe.

The contractor, Daniel Climie of Shrewsbury, started work at Barnstaple in 1864, but was almost immediately replaced by Messrs William & John Pickering. By August 1866 the line from Norton Fitzwarren to Wiveliscombe was staked out, but then Messrs Pickering had to discharge the navvies as the D&SR was unable to make cash payments for the work. The stoppage was only for a few days and we read in the *Somerset County Gazette* that on 24th August a navvy who had arrived at Wiveliscombe fell ill with cholera, at that time the disease being prevalent throughout the country. Another navvy caught it and in an effort to prevent it spreading, pitch fires were lit in every street. Fortunately the threatened epidemic was curtailed and few went down with the disease.

The inhabitants of Milverton had anticipated that the navvies would have proved an unruly lot, and were agreeably surprised that their conduct was exemplary and the increase of thefts and assaults insufficient to need more than one police sergeant, the *Somerset County Gazette* believing the record was due to the example set by the 'executive managers'.

This peaceful scene was suddenly shattered when, without warning, on 29th September 1866, Messrs Pickering paid off all labourers and suspended work for an indefinite period. This step had to be taken because the contractors once again had not been paid and naturally declined to proceed at their own risk. The works lay dormant for almost four years until 11th May 1870 when the D&SR Directors met to give the contract to John Langham Reed. This meeting was memorable for the fact that Eugenius Birch, who had been dismissed as the company's engineer some 17 months previously, because he was incapable of efficiently superintending completion of the line, attended the meeting and when asked to leave, refused, only going under protest when the Directors threatened to send for the police. His office was filled by Richard Hassard.

Milverton, view Down in broad gauge days before doubling. At the far end of the platform, notice the disc and crossbar signal at danger. Beside it is the flag signal for indicating 'Caution'. *Author's Collection*

In October 1870 Arthur Moore, secretary of the B&ER which was to work the line, complained that the branch was defective with poor ballasting, unsatisfactory masonry, a dangerously steep approach to Milverton station, aged fencing and defective and uncreosoted sleepers. In March the D&SR replied saying that since the receipt of the letter, the line had been approved by the Board of Trade inspector 'and no question of safety can now arise'.

On 8th June 1871 the line opened from Norton Junction, as Norton Fitzwarren was then called, to Wiveliscombe, with an intermediate station at Milverton. There was no special ceremony, but the leading inhabitants of Milverton and Wiveliscombe were taken to Taunton in a saloon carriage and entertained in a marquee on the lawn of C Daniel of North Town. The first train left Wiveliscombe at 7.00am and carried 'a moderate amount of passengers', the locomotive being decorated with flowers and evergreens. It was greeted by a crowd at Milverton and later trains were filled. No bells rang at Wiveliscombe and although the shops were closed, there were few people about, most having gone to Milverton for the celebrations. The latter town was elaborately decorated. By the turnpike gate was a double arch with 'Success to the Devon & Somerset Railway' worked in flowers, other arches bearing similar legends. Two bands were playing, unfortunately in close proximity, and rural sports were held. Sixty quarter-pound packets of tea were given to the oldest and poorest women in the parish, and the pupils of the National School, numbering nearly 300, each received a penny.

The B&ER gave a breakdown of the weekly expenses of working the line:

	£	s	d
Share of expenses at Norton Junction, of signalmen, signals and stores	1	10	0
Station work at Milverton and Wiveliscombe and working block	13	10	0
Stores and stationery at Milverton and Wiveliscombe	5	0	0
Wages and clothing of guard	1	7	6

Use of carriage stock:	pence per mile
First class and composite	1½
Second class	1¼
Third class	1
Vans	1
Horse boxes	¾
Carriage trucks	½
Covered wagons	7/16
Open trucks	3/8
Sheets	1/16

Coupled tank locomotives: for a train of not more than 6 vehicles 10d per mile and ½d per vehicle for each vehicle above 6.

Time demonstrated that it was a case of cheap proving dear. The permanent way supplied by Messrs Pickering was of poor quality and 84 rails had to be replaced,

though about half were re-used after the defective end had been cut off. A further 680 rails displayed signs of failure. The permanent way work and repair of fence kept busy a foreman and two gangs, each of four men whose weekly wages and tool costs totalled £9.

The line was extended to Barnstaple on 1st November 1873. Subsequent history was less exciting. The last broad gauge train ran over the line on Saturday 14th May 1881, the line being converted on Sunday and Monday. The company was purchased by the GWR in 1901. It was considered important, Great Western cartographers marking it with a broad red line denoting main line status such as was used for Paddington to Penzance, as opposed to the narrow line used for branches. With the increase of people going on holiday, problems were experienced in the 1930s when working heavy traffic over the line on Saturdays. Automatic token exchangers were installed so that non-stop trains could run through stations at higher speed than when the token was exchanged manually. The apparatus consisted of a combined picking up and setting down pillar, (except at Milverton where the single line began), and was placed on the left hand side of the line. This patent apparatus had been designed c.1903 by Alfred Whitaker, locomotive superintendent of the Somerset & Dorset Joint Railway. Manufactured by the Railway Signal Company, it was modified to take GWR pattern token pouches. On receiving 'Line clear' and withdrawing the token from its instrument, the signalman placed it in the delivery clip and set the arm of the exchange apparatus at right angles to the track ready for the exchange to be made. After collection by the train, the arm swung parallel with the track and became locked into position in order to give sufficient clearance to the rolling stock.

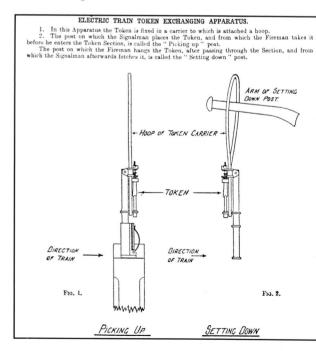

Diagram from the *General Appendix to the Rule Book* (GWR, 1936)

Milverton station, view Down after doubling.

Author's Collection

Milverton, with its signalbox and neat garden to the left.

Author's Collection

The equipment on the engine consisted of a receiving jaw and delivery clip fixed on the end of a slide which worked through a guide on the bunker or tender. This slide was operated by means of a handle which locked the gear in either the 'in' or 'out' position. After passing a distant signal, the fireman placed the token in the clip and as the locomotive approached the exchange pillar, pushed the slide out. As soon as the exchange was made, the slide had to be withdrawn in order that the platform was not fouled. Trains booked to stop at a station or Stop Board, exchanged the token by hand and when using this method, speed was limited to 10 mph, though this restriction was sometimes broken and the token caught on a coal pick while the other token was dropped on the platform. The automatic exchange apparatus was not an unqualified success as it was not entirely reliable, engines shaking sideways under load or a depression of a rail, making the catcher miss. On one occasion a token flew off the catcher into a field of wheat and was lost for a time. Other problems arose such as the time when a driver was cleaning and oiling the catcher on shed, was called forward on to the turntable, forgot to return the catcher to the running position and bent it.

To improve running, the line from Norton Fitzwarren to Milverton was doubled in 1937; at the same time the junction at Norton Fitzwarren was slightly repositioned so that it left directly from the main line instead of from the Minehead branch. The route was busy during World War Two, but with the increase in road transport afterwards, became uneconomic and closed on 1st October 1966.

West of Norton Fitzwarren, the D&SR ran parallel with the Exeter line for a quarter of a mile before rising on a gradient of 1 in 70 to Milverton. The original station, with its brick-built offices, was on the south side of the line, an Up platform with a timber waiting-shelter being added when the passing loop was laid in about 1880. The goods station was built conveniently next to the passenger station. As the station was on an incline of 1 in 60, when an engine was detached for shunting, the brake of the guard's van had to be applied, enough wagon brakes put down, and sprags used to prevent the train moving. A sufficient number of sprags for this purpose was kept between the running lines.

Inwards traffic was chiefly made up of coal, fertilisers and livestock. Horses for hunting were usually loaded and unloaded on the passenger platform unless the owner warned that they were nervous. Outwards traffic was mainly in the form of sugar beet. The station closed to goods on 30th September 1963. In 1952 the staff consisted of stationmaster, two signalmen and a lad porter, but latterly it came under the jurisdiction of the Wiveliscombe stationmaster. The signalmen at Milverton worked the most overtime on the branch as their box was the first to open and the last to close, but they welcomed the extra money. As at many stations, there were tales of guards being left behind. Certainly on at least one occasion a taxi driver at Milverton was telephoned and asked to collect the guard whom the train had left behind at Wiveliscombe.

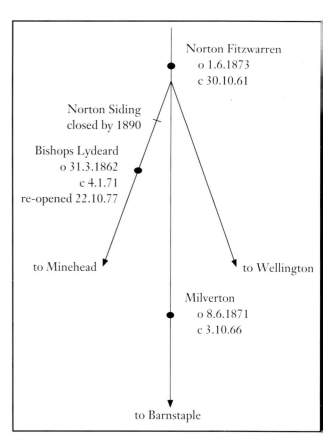

Diagrammatic map of the route from Norton Fitzwarren to Milverton and Bishops Lydeard

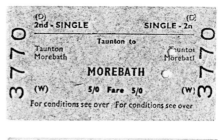

78

6. Taunton to Bishops Lydeard

Back in 1845 a line was proposed to run from the B&ER at Bridgwater, through Minehead to Ilfracombe, ships sailing from there to Ireland. This particular scheme proved abortive, but in the 1850s a line was proposed to link Bridgwater with Watchet, but then the alternative of a branch from Norton Fitzwarren seemed more feasible. Influential landowners met at Williton on 9th July 1856 to promote a railway from that district and the mineral railway then in course of construction from the Somerset Ironworks on the Brendon Hills, to the B&ER. A few weeks later, on 26th October, a meeting was held in the Guildhall, Taunton, for the purpose of promoting the West Somerset Railway. Those attending pledged themselves to support the Directors and engineer, giving them *carte blanche* to do what they thought fit. The engineer was, in fact, I K Brunel and it was to prove one of his final undertakings. Some landowners' agents made unreasonable claims for compensation and together with other increased costs, caused the estimated expenses to rise by £20,000 to £150,000. The extra cash was not easily raised, but at last contracts were advertised and that with George Furness of London signed on 5th April 1859. The ceremony of turning the first sod took place at Crowcombe on 7th April the same year, work starting in earnest three days later. Not all financial difficulties had been solved and work proceeded slowly, it taking nearly three years before the 14½ miles of broad gauge line were opened. During 1859 the company lost its engineer, with Brunel's death on 15th September; the office was filled by his chief assistant, R P Brereton.

No 3833 (Newport, Ebbw Junction), a freight engine, unusually heads an express to Paignton on a Saturday in August 1947, suggesting that there was a shortage of motive power. At platform 1, 'Mogul' No 6343 is in charge of a through Paddington to Minehead express. To aid signalmen, Minehead trains carried a disc with an 'M', while those to Barnstaple bore a 'B'.
Clive Bousfield

MINEHEAD BRANCH.

Single Line, Bishop's Lydeard to Dunster, worked by Electric Token. Crossing Places are Crowcombe, Leigh Bridge, Williton, Kentsford, and Blue Anchor. Leigh Bridge and Kentsford are opened as required on Saturdays only. Washford is a Staff Station. Intermediate Token Instrument at Watchet. When necessary a Train (not conveying passengers) may be placed in the Siding at Watchet or Washford for another train or trains to pass in the same or opposite direction.

DOWN TRAINS. — WEEK DAYS.

M.P. Mileage from Padd.	Dist. from T'nt'n	STATIONS.	Ruling Gradient.	Point-to-Point Times	Allow for Stop.	Allow for Start.	K Freight.	B Passenger. MSO	B Passenger.	K Freight.		B Passenger.	K Freight.	B Passenger.	B Passenger.
M. C.	M. C.			Mins.	Mins.	Mins.	arr. dep.	arr. dep.	arr. dep.	arr. dep.		arr. dep.	arr. dep.	arr. dep.	arr. dep.
163 11	—	TAUNTON	—	—	—	2	— 5 45	— 6 25	— 7 28	— 7 40		9 10 9 11	— 10 0	10 25 10 26	11 55 11
165 8	1 77	Norton Fitzwarren	—	5	1	1	—	6 30	7 32 7 33	7 47		9 17 9 18	10 7	10 32 10 33	12 3 12
168 20	5 9	Bishop's Lydeard	93 R.	10	1	2	6 2 6 12	6 36 6 37	7 39 7 40			9 25 9 26	10 17 10 17	10 40 10 41	12 14 12
172 10	8 79	Crowcombe	80 R.	13	1	1	6 22 6 28	6 44 6 45	7 47 7 48	8 11 X 8 18			10 55 11 15		
174 8	10 77	Leigh Bridge	93 F.	—	—	—	C R	6 50 6 51	7 53 7 54			9 31 9 32	11 25 11 40	10 47 10 48	12 20 12
174 64	11 53	Stogumber	98 F.	7	2	1	6 43 7 15	7 0 7 0	8 0 X8 3	8 36 X 8 50		9 39 9 43	11 51 11 13	10 55 10 59	1227 X 12
178 6	14 75	Williton	91 F.	8	2	1	6 57 7 0	7 4 7 6	8 7 8 8	8 57		9 47 9 49	1 21 1 30	11 4 11 7	12 34 12
179 64	16 53	Watchet	147 F.	5	1	2	7 21 7 30								
180 40	17 29	Kentsford	82 R.	—	—	—		7 12 7 13	8 14 8 15			9 55 9 56	1 38 1 50	11 14 11 15	12 41 12
182 11	19 0	Washford	76 R.	7	1	1	7 40 8 40	7 17 7 18	8 19 8 20			10 0 10 1	1 58 2 10	11 20 11 26	12 46 12
184 34	21 23	Blue Anchor	66 F.	6	1	1	8 48 8 55	7 22 7 23	8 24 8 25			10 5 10 6	2 16 2 30	11 30 11 31	12 52 12
186 21	23 10	Dunster	80 F.	4	1	1	9 0 9 10	7 28	8 25			10 10 —	2 36 —	11 35 —	12 57 —
187 71	24 60	MINEHEAD	224 F.	4		1	9 15								

DOWN TRAINS. — WEEK DAYS—continued.

STATIONS.	A 9.40 a.m. Paddington Passenger. SO June 21st to Sept. 20th.	B Passenger. SO	B Passenger. K	A 11.30 a.m. Paddington Passenger. SO June 21st to Sept. 20th.	B Passenger. SO	B Passenger. SUSPENDED	Passenger. 80 June 21st to Sept. 20th.	B Passenger.	B Passenger.	B Passenger. FO		B Passenger.
	arr. dep.	arr. dep.	arr. dep.	arr. dep.	arr. dep.	arr. dep.	arr. dep.	arr. dep.	arr. dep.	arr. dep.		arr. dep.
TAUNTON	12 29 12 37	— 12 42	— 2 5	2 7 2 2	— 2 30	— 2 50	— 3 30	— 5 5	— 6 30	— 7 30		— 9 5
Norton F.	C S	12 46 12 47	2 10 2 11	2 2 2 30	2 35 2 38	2 55 2 50	3 35 3 36	5 9 5 10	6 34 6 35	7 34 7 35		9 10 9 11
Bishop's L.	C S	12 56 X7 1	2 17 2 18	2 25 X2 26	2 45 2 46	3 3 3 4	3 43 3 41	5 16 X5 17	6 41 6 42	7 42 7 43		9 18 9 20
Crowcombe	C S X	1 8 1 9	2 25 X2 26	2 47 X2 52	3 3 12	3 53 X4 2	3 58 X4 2	5 22 5 23	6 49 6 50	7 50 7 51		9 28 9 30
Leigh Bridge	C S	1 14 1 15	2 32 2 33		3 2 3 3	3 17 3 18	4 5 4 6	5 30 5 31	6 56 6 57	7 56 7 57		9 36 9 37
Stogumber	C S	1 21 1 26	2 39 2 42		3 9 3 12	3 24 3 25	4 12 4 15	5 37 X5 40	7 3 X7 8	8 3 8 6		9 43 X9 47
Williton	C S	1 30 1 34	2 46 2 48		3 16 3 18	3 31 3 33	4 19 4 21	5 44 5 45	7 12 7 13	8 10 8 11		9 51 9 53
Watchet												
Kentsford												
Washford	C S	1 40 1 42	2 54 2 55	C S	3 24 3 25	3 39 3 40	4 28 4 29	5 51 5 52	7 19 7 20	8 17 8 18		10 0 10 1
Blue Anchor	C S	1 46 X1 51	2 59 3 0	C S	3 29 X3 32	3 44 X3 46	4 33 X4 36	5 56 5 57	7 24 7 25	8 22 X8 23		10 5 10 6
Dunster	C S	1 55 1 57	3 4 3 5	3 17	3 36 3 37	3 50 3 51	4 40 4 41	6 1 6 2	7 29 7 32	8 27 8 28		10 10 10 11
MINEHEAD	1 25	2 2 —	3 9	3 21	3 41	3 55	4 45	6 5	7 38	8 32		10 15 —

MINEHEAD BRANCH—continued.

UP TRAINS. — WEEK DAYS.

STATIONS.	Ruling Gradient.	Point-to-Point Times	Allow for Stop.	Allow for Start.	B Passenger. MSO	A Passenger.	B Passenger.	B Passenger.	B Passenger.	B Passenger. SO	K Freight.	B Passenger.		A Paddington Passenger. SO June 21st to Sept. 20th.
		Mins.	Mins.	Mins.	arr. dep.	arr. dep.	arr. dep.	arr. dep.	arr. dep.	arr. dep.	arr. dep.	arr. dep.		arr. dep.
MINEHEAD	224 R.	—	—	1	— 7 35	— 8 25	— 9 10	— 11 15	— 12 5	— 12 35		— 1 40		— 2
Dunster	80 R.	4	1	1	7 39 7 40	8 29 8 30	9 14 9 16	11 19 11 20	12 9 12 10	12 39 12 40		1 44 1 45		C S
Blue Anchor	66 R.	4	1	1	7 44 7 45	C S	9 20 9 22	11 24 11 25	12 13 12 15	12 44 X12 47		1 49 X1 50		C S
Washford	93 F.	6		1	7 50 7 51	C S	9 27 9 28	11 30 11 31	12 21 12 21	12 52 12 53		1 55 1 56		C S
Kentsford	76 F.													
Watchet	147 F.	8	2	1	7 56 7 57	8 43 8 44	9 37 9 39	11 36 11 38	12 20 12 22	12 58 12 59				
Williton	91 R.	5	1	2	8 1 X8 4	8 48 8 51	9 41 X9 45	11 42 11 45	12 31 X12 34	1 3 1 4	1 12 X 1 27	2 6 2 7		C S
Stogumber	98 R.	6	1	2	8 10 8 11		9 51 9 52	11 51 11 52	12 41 12 41	1 12 1 13		2 15 2 16		
Leigh Bridge	93 R.													
Crowcombe	93 R.	8	1	1	8 16 8 17	C S	9 58 9 59	11 58 11 59	12 48 X12 53	1 19 1 20	C S	2 22 X2 27		C S
Bish'p's L'deard	80 R.	9	2	1	8 24 8 25	C S	10 6 10 8	12 6 X12 8	1 0 1 1	1 27 1 28	1 58 2 25	2 34 2 35		C S
Norton F.	93 R.	8	1	1	8 30 8 31	R L	10 13 10 15	12 14 12 16	1 12 12 16	1 33	2 34	2 40 2 41		C S
TAUNTON	—			5	8 35	9 20	10 20 —	12 21	1 20	1 37	2 40	2 45		3 12 3

UP TRAINS. — WEEK DAYS—continued.

STATIONS.	B Passenger. SO	K Freight.	B Passenger. SUSPENDED	B Passenger.	K Freight.	B Passenger.	B Passenger. SO	B Passenger. SO June 21st to Sept. 20th.	B Passenger.	B Passenger. FO		
	arr. dep.	arr. dep.	arr. dep.	arr. dep.	arr. dep.	arr. dep.	arr. dep.	arr. dep.	arr. dep.	arr. dep.		
MINEHEAD	— 3 20	— 11 40	— 3 35	— 4 25	— 5 10	— 6 5	— 6 35	— 8 10	— 9 15			
Dunster	3 24 3 25	11 45 4 10	3 39 3 40	4 29 4 30	3 55 T3 15	6 10 6 11	6 39 6 40	8 14 8 16	9 19 9 21			
Blue Anchor	3 30 X3 31	C R	3 45 X3 47	4 34 X4 35	4 25	6 15 6 16	6 46 6 46	8 20 X8 24	9 27 9 27			
Washford	3 56 3 57	1 20 1 38	3 53 3 55	4 40 4 41	3 25 3 41	6 21 6 22	6 51 6 53	8 29 8 30	9 32 9 33			
Kentsford												
Watchet	3 42 3 44	1 46 2 45	4 0 4 1	4 46 4 48	3 49 4 15	6 27 6 28	6 58 6 59	8 35 8 36	9 40 9 10			
Williton	3 48 3 51	2 53 3 30	4 9 4 13	4 52 4 55	4 35	6 32 6 35	7 7 7 8	8 40 8 43	9 44 X9 50			
Stogumber	3 57 3 58	—	4 19 4 20	5 1 5 2	C R	6 41 6 42	7 13 7 14	8 50 8 51	9 57 9 58			
Leigh Bridge	C S	C S			C R							
Crowcombe	4 4 4 5	C S	4 27 4 29	5 8 5 9	5 25	6 48 X6 51	7 21 7 22	8 57 8 58	10 4 10 5			
Bishop's L.	4 12 4 13	4 0 4 20	4 36 4 38	5 16 5 18	5 5 5 25	6 56 6 57	7 28 7 29	9 6 9 6	10 12 10 13			
Norton F.	4 18 4 20	4 20 R	4 44 4 46	5 23 5 25	5 34	7 6 7 7	7 35 7 36	9 12 9 12	10 18 10 19			
TAUNTON	4 25	4 35	4 50	5 30	5 40	6 11	7 41	9 17	10 24			

‡ —Runs 2 minutes later from Williton on Saturdays.   K —Will not run on Saturdays, June 21st to Sept. 20th, inclusive.   Y —Extended to Paddington on Saturdays.

Extract from the GWR working timetable for summer 1947

The line was sufficiently complete for a locomotive to travel over it on 6th March 1862 and the undertaking was visited by the Board of Trade Inspecting Officer two days later. His report was satisfactory, indeed some of the original rails lasted at Crowcombe until 1923. The ceremonial opening was held on 29th March when a beflagged train of first class coaches carrying the Directors and their friends left Taunton station immediately after the departure of the 1.50pm Down express. The line opened to the public two days later. Four trains ran in each direction and two on Sundays. At first the line was only used by passenger trains, the goods sheds not being ready until August.

The line was extended to Minehead on 16th July 1874 and four years later it was recommended that the branch be converted to standard gauge as soon as possible to save the cost of transferring goods on to broad gauge wagons at Taunton and also to relieve the broad gauge wagon shortage which was becoming acute since the GWR did not wish to build new vehicles in view of the eventual total abolition of this gauge. The 22¼ miles of track were attacked by 500 men in seven gangs of 70 at daybreak on Sunday 29th October 1882 with such vigour that soon after midday a standard gauge special with the Divisional Engineer and Traffic Superintendent was able to get through to Minehead. Next day one passenger train ran in each direction and on Tuesday morning the normal service was resumed.

The Minehead Railway was taken over by the GWR in 1897 after that company had acquired all its capital. The GWR had to reach its new possession over West Somerset Railway metals, for the latter retained its independence until 1922.

The opening of Butlin's holiday camp at Minehead in 1962 increased summer traffic and as many as 2,000 long distance passengers were handled on a peak summer Saturday. Freight on the branch ceased under the Taunton Concentration Scheme. From 26th February 1968 economies were made on the branch when, except at terminal stations, passengers obtained their tickets from the guard. Even so, the line was not thought to be economic and the last BR train ran on 2nd January 1971. Fortunately this was not the end of the story and the line was re-opened by a new West Somerset Railway Company, Bishops Lydeard becoming its eastern terminus.

Bishops Lydeard station, sited about half a mile from the village, originally had only a single platform on the south side and, as on the Milverton line, the goods shed was conveniently sited next to the passenger station. To facilitate working, a passing loop and Up platform were brought into use on 2nd July 1906. In 1943 a Ministry of Works siding was added. As the station was on an incline of 1 in 85 falling towards Norton Fitzwarren, before a goods engine was detached from its train, the brake in the guard's van had to be securely applied and also sufficient wagon brakes and sprags used to prevent the train moving as at Milverton. Six sprags, ten yards apart, had to be kept between the main lines.

Bishops Lydeard, view Up, c.1962.

Lens of Sutton

A Minehead to Taunton train comprising a 'B' set, hauled by No 2267 (Taunton) with an ex-Railway Operating Division tender, passes Silk Mill crossing in February 1947. War Department diesel 0-4-0 No 72334 shunts in Blinkhorn Sidings.　*Roger Venning*

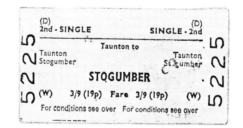

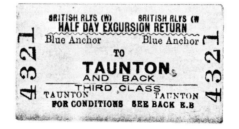

7. The Motive Power Scene: 1930s to 1960s

Pride of the shed was its 'Castles' – No 5003 *Lulworth Castle* and No 5077 *Eastnor Castle*, renamed *Fairey Battle* in October 1940. These generally worked the 7.30am to Bristol, or 7.20am to Exeter. At one period during World War Two, Taunton had three 'Castles', the extra being No 5078 *Beaufort* sent when raids on London made life difficult for staff at Old Oak Common. No 5078 worked the 2.00pm Plymouth to Paddington, (4.16pm ex-Taunton) and the 9.05pm Paddington to Penzance, the sleeping car express which was derailed at Norton Fitzwarren in 1940, though this was before Taunton men started working this train. The 'Castle' came off at Taunton and the train was re-engined.

One Taunton man vividly recalls polishing, in the mid-thirties, the very long nameplate of 'Castle' No 4016 *Knight of the Golden Fleece*. He also remembers that when No 5958 *Knolton Hall* arrived new in 1936, the paint appeared as if it had been left in a dusty atmosphere while still wet. Certainly the paintwork was very rough and the chargeman ordered all the Taunton cleaners to scour it with brick dust to give it a pristine appearance.

Taunton had three 'Stars': No 4026, un-named, but originally *Japanese Monarch*, No 4054 *Princess Charlotte* and No 4056 *Princess Margaret*; these usually headed stopping trains from Taunton to Bristol or Exeter. The three 'Bulldog' 4-4-0s, No 3443 *Chaffinch*, No 3361 (un-named) and No 3444 *Cormorant*, were mostly rostered as East End coach shunter and standby bank engine for working from Taunton to Savernake as, until the British Railways era, this class was the only type authorised to double-head 'Kings' as it would have been wasteful to use a 4-6-0 when it was a case of just a few tons over the limit. Sometimes 'Bulldogs' worked passenger trains to Minehead and Yeovil. A certain element among the footplate crews gained amusement from adding 'IN' as a prefix and 'AX' as suffix to the name of 'Duke' class No 3283 making it read 'INCOME TAX'.

63XX and 73XX class 2-6-0s worked almost exclusively on the Barnstaple branch passenger and freight trains and during the summer months ran through to Ilfracombe. Some engines of this class were fitted with apparatus for picking up the train tablet. Over the

No 5003 *Lulworth Castle* (Taunton) at platform 7 in charge of a stopping train to Bristol in September 1947. Wheel-tappers stand beside the leading coach.
Roger Venning

RUNNING TIMES FOR RETURN BANK ENGINES.

Totnes to Dainton	‡10 minutes.	Wellington to Norton Fitzwarren	‡10 minutes.
Dainton to Aller Junction	‡ 6 minutes.	Norton Fitzwarren to Taunton	‡ 5 minutes.
Dainton to Totnes	‡10 minutes.	East Anstey to Dulverton	8 minutes.
Whiteball to Wellington	‡8 minutes.		

‡—One minute less for 31XX and 51XX class of Engines.

CONVEYANCE OF PASSENGER STOCK BY GOODS TRAIN.

The tare weight of each vehicle must be ascertained and calculated as every 10 tons equalling a Class 3 loaded wagon, e.g., a passenger coach weighing 20 tons should be counted as two Class 3 wagons.

In dealing with fractions of 10 tons, 5 tons and under to be dropped and over 5 tons to be treated as 10 tons, e.g., a passenger coach weighing 25 tons 15 cwt. should be counted as 30 tons, equalling three Class 3 wagons; similarly a passenger coach weighing 24 tons 19 cwt. should be counted as 20 tons, equalling two Class 3 wagons.

Coaching stock (passenger coaches and passenger brake vans) must not be conveyed on freight trains which have to pass two or more Divisions, without the consent of the Controls concerned.

Freight Trains scheduled in the Marshalling Instructions for the conveyance of coaching stock are excepted from these arrangements.

BANKING AND SHUNTING ENGINES.

STATIONS.	Engine No	Starting Times.	AUTHORIZED HOURS. Mon.	Tues.	Wed.	Thur.	Fri.	Sat.	Sun.	Total hours per week.	REMARKS.
			PAS SEN GER.								
Taunton	1	5.30 a.m.	18½	—	—	—	—	—	—	18½	Shunting
	1	2.30 a.m.	—	22	22	22	22	22	—	110	
	2	6.30 a.m.	17	—	—	—	—	—	—	17	
	2	6 45 a.m	—	16¾	16¾	16¾	16¾	16¾	—	83¾	
	3	3.15 a.m	—	1	1	1	1	1	1	6	
	—	7.30 a.m	—	—	—	—	—	—	13½	13½	
Exeter	1	5 30 a.m.	18½	—	—	—	—	—	—	18½	Shunting.
	1	12. 0 nt.	—	24	24	24	24	24	6	126	
	2	7. 0 a.m.	2¼	2¼	2¼	2¼	2¼	2¼	—	13½	
	2	4. 0 p.m.	7½	7½	7½	7½	7½	7½	—	45	
	—	8.15 a.m.	1	1	1	1	1	1	—	6	Shunting, train engines
	—	8.45 p.m.	2¼	2¼	2¼	2¼	2¼	2¼	—	13½	
	1	1 30 p.m.	2¼	2¼	2¼	2¼	2¼	2¼	—	13½	
	1	8.45 a.m.	—	—	—	—	—	—	2½	2½	Shunting
	1	2. 0 p.m.	—	—	—	—	—	—	1¼	1¼	
	1	7.45 p.m.	—	—	—	—	—	—	3¾	3¾	
	—	11. 0 a.m.	—	—	—	—	—	—	2½	2½	Shunting, train engines
	—	3.15 p.m.	—	—	—	—	—	—	4¼	4¼	
Newton Abbot	1	2.30 a.m.	24	24	24	24	24	24	24	168	Shunting.
	2	5.45 a.m.	2	2	2	2	2	2	—	12	Train engine.
	3	8.30 a.m.	12½	12½	12½	12½	12½	12½	—	75	Shunting.
	4	5.20 p.m.	½	½	½	½	½	½	—	3	Train engine.
	2	7.30 a.m.	—	—	—	—	—	—	3½	3½	Shunting, train engines.
	3	11. 0 a.m.	—	—	—	—	—	—	3½	3½	

REFUGE SIDINGS AND RUNNING LOOPS.

STATION.	Refuge Siding.	Running Loop.	No. of 10-ton Wagons Siding or Loop holds in addition to Engine and Van.
DOWN			
Somerton	—	1	86
Athelney	—	1	87
Highbridge	—	1	60
Bridgwater	—	1	63
Durston	1	—	50
Creech Junction	1	—	58
Norton Fitzwarren to Victory Crossing	—	1	155
Wellington	1	—	48
Wellington	—	1X	61
Whiteball Tunnel	1	—	44
Whiteball and Burlescombe Loop	—	1	140‡
Sampford Peverell Halt	—	1X	85
Tiverton Junction	—	1X	52
Tiverton Junction	1	—	51
Cullompton	1	—	52
Cullompton	—	1X	48
Hele and Bradninch	—	1	86
Stoke Canon	—	1X	46
Cowley Bridge Jct. and Exeter East	—	1	165*
Exminster	—	1	79
Exminster	—	1X	98
Dawlish Warren	—	1X	75
Hackney	—	1	79
Aller Junction	—	1	64
Dainton	1	—	32
Totnes	—	1	56
Torre	1	—	35
Goodrington	—	1	39
Churston	1	—	40
Longdown	—	1	47

STATION.	Refuge Siding.	Running Loop.	No. of 10-ton Wagons Siding or Loop holds in addition to Engine and Van.
UP			
Goodrington	—	1	64
Dainton	1	—	27
Newton Abbot	1	—	44
Hackney (Down Side)	—	1	76
Hackney (Up Side)	—	1	70
Teignmouth	1	—	52
Dawlish Warren	—	1X	80
Exminster	—	1X	80
Exminster	1	—	60
Stoke Canon	—	1X	80
Silverton	1	—	32
Hele and Bradninch	—	1	86
Cullompton	—	1X	54
Tiverton Junction	—	1X	45
Tiverton Junction	1	—	70
Sampford Peverell Halt	—	1X	80
Burlescombe	1	—	41
Wellington	—	1X	67
Norton Fitzwarren	1	—	60
Creech Junction	1	—	55
Durston	1	—	50
Bridgwater	—	1	66
Highbridge	1	—	60
Athelney	—	1	88
Somerton	—	1	86
Molland	1	—	28
East Anstey	1	—	28
Venn Cross	1	—	28
Christow	1	—	45
DOWN OR UP			
Taunton West Jct. to Silk Milk Crossing	—	1	137

‡—Whiteball Tunnel End—clear of Catch Point to Relief Line Advanced Starting Signal .. .. 43 Wagons.
Between Whiteball Tunnel Relief Line Advanced Starting Signal and Burlescombe Relief Line Home Signal 97 Wagons.
*—Cowley Bridge Junction to intermediate connection 78 wagons in addition to engine and van. Intermediate connection to exit West end 60 wagons in addition to engine and van. X—Platform Lines

Banking engine information from the GWR service timetable appendices, 1945

The 8.30am Plymouth to Paddington train about to leave Taunton behind No 3443 *Chaffinch* (Taunton) and No 4042 *Prince Albert* (Bristol, Bath Road) on 11th September 1947. The latter took over from a failed 'King' at Exeter and *Chaffinch* was added at Taunton to assist over the undulating road to Reading. (This is the same train as that on page 33). *Roger Venning*

Barnstaple branch they were permitted to haul a maximum of 10 coaches, double-heading not being allowed without special dispensation such as was given for working the Royal Train. One Taunton 63XX on banking duty during World War Two made 13 trips between midnight and 7.00am and then had to return to shed as the efforts of climbing to Whiteball had cleared the tender of coal. No 4321 was a Taunton 2-6-0 with a number very easy to remember.

2-8-0s Nos 2814 and 2822 were allocated to Taunton specifically for working the Banbury goods. 2251 class 0-6-0s were used on various branch passenger and goods trains such as the 7.24am passenger to Barnstaple and the 6.52pm to Yeovil. They worked many Minehead trains, a full tender lasting all day. No 2267 was the last engine of this class at Taunton with a pole, instead of screw, reverser. No 2214 was a superb engine, while No 2213 was inadvertently fitted with a 225-lb safety valve instead of a 200-lb one. Consequently she was a strong engine and liked by drivers. Eventually the fault was spotted and the valve changed. This class largely replaced those of the 'Dean Goods' type of which Nos 2416, 2472, 2527, 2537, 2578 were shedded at Taunton in the 1930s.

2-6-2T No 3184 was sent to Taunton, but as it was a 'Red' engine and not allowed by its weight to run on the Minehead branch, it was replaced by a 51XX class engine of the same wheel arrangement. 41XX and 51XX class engines from Taunton shed were originally used for banking duties between Wellington and Whiteball. If assisting a Down freight from Taunton, an engine was required to be coupled at the rear as far as Wellington where it ran uncoupled to Whiteball signalbox. As more of these types were stationed at Taunton they took over some of the passenger trains to Minehead, especially on summer Saturdays when loads exceeded the 260 tons maximum for 45XX and 55XX class 2-6-2Ts. Weight restrictions kept the 41XX and 51XX engines from the Barnstaple line.

The 45XX and 55XX classes worked both passenger and freight trains on the Minehead, Yeovil and Chard branches and sometimes on the Barnstaple line – such as the 6.30am South Molton freight and the 7.40am Dulverton goods. Some members of the class were fitted with train tablet catchers.

No 3184, Taunton West End pilot, moving coaches to sidings in summer 1939. Notice the advertisement for the *Sunday Pictorial* above the nameboard.
Bob Franklin

'Metro' class 2-4-0Ts Nos 3582, 3590 and 3591 were used during the very early years of Blinkhorn Sidings, an engine of this type with a Taunton driver and fireman shunting until the United States Transportation Corps obtained its own 0-6-0 side tank locomotives for which Taunton shed carried out light repairs and washing out duties. Early in 1946 the War Department took over the site and used its own locomotives including Bagnall 0-6-0ST No WD 75165 and Drewry 0-4-0 No WD 72334. Nos 3582 and 3590 were also used during World War Two on auto train working to Bridgwater, Venn Cross, Castle Cary and Hendford – the latter for workers at Westland Aircraft Limited. One member of the class was used as the West End carriage shunter.

57XX class 0-6-0PTs were used mainly on branch passenger and freight trains, mostly over the Chard and Minehead lines. Some engines of this wheel arrangement were antiquated, such as Nos 1760, 1899, 2708, 2748 and 2755, and were used for shunting until withdrawn when they were replaced by engines of the 57XX class. The smaller 2021 class Nos 2038, 2088, 2116 and 2127 were used almost exclusively at Bridgwater.

Ex-Burry Port & Gwendraeth Valley Railway 0-6-0ST No 2194 *Kidwelly* came from Weymouth, worked on the 5.35am goods to Bridgwater, shunted there all day and returned to Taunton light at about 10.00pm. It was mostly used for shunting duties at Dunball Wharf, north of Bridgwater, coping with the very sharp curves and weight restrictions. Taunton men worked this trip out

and back, putting off some traffic at Bridgwater. When *Kidwelly* was undergoing repair, an 0-6-0ST, usually No 1363, was borrowed from Laira shed, Plymouth.

Another Welsh engine was No 1338, an ex-Cardiff Railway 0-4-0ST. It was transferred to Taunton in September 1943 for shunting at Bridgwater Docks and was the only Cardiff Railway engine to stray far from home. From February 1955 it was the CR's sole survivor. It left Taunton in June 1960. Its interesting feature was J Hawthorn Kitson's valve gear, a modified Walschaert's pattern, having the link above the running plate. When in motion, the valve gear went up and down 'like a grasshopper'. Its coal bunker was alongside the boiler and at the rear of the cab was a removable panel to ease the replacement of tubes which could not be reached from the front of the locomotive. On returning from Bridgwater to Taunton one Saturday, the fireman put his shovel out through this hole and waved it sideways as if rowing the engine along. No 5 *Portishead*, an ex-London, Brighton & South Coast Railway 'Terrier' class 0-6-0T which arrived on the GWR via the Weston, Clevedon & Portishead Railway, came to Taunton in December 1948, remaining until January 1950 when it was transferred to Newton Abbot. It had no injectors and water was fed into the boiler by an axle pump. It shunted at Bridgwater and if water became low, the engine was cut off from the wagons and run up and down the sidings to pump the water boiler up. It was a remarkable engine – when stripped down no wear was apparent.

No 3582 (of Taunton shed despite 'SBZ' – St Blazey – on the frame) in the coaling queue at Taunton shed, September 1947. Coach No 6980 was a 'B' set brake composite built in 1930.
Roger Venning

No 2038 (Taunton) with a match truck, shunts in Taunton East yard, June 1947. Notice the tarpaulin to keep the sun (or a cool breeze?) from the cab.
Roger Venning

The second part of the Manchester to Torquay & Paignton express, composed of LMS stock and hauled by No 5033 *Broughton Castle* (Chester), passes Dunball on 20th September 1947. The line from a quarry towards Dunball Wharf, the haunt of *Kidwelly*, crosses the main lines on the level.

Pursey Short

On Saturday 12th May 1945, ex-Burry Port & Gwendraeth Valley Railway 0-6-0ST No 194 *Kidwelly* nears Creech St Michael as it returns light engine from Bridgwater to its home shed. *Pursey Short*

No 1338, sub-shedded at Bridgwater, on the goods loop behind Taunton locomotive shed, waiting for signals, April 1947. *Roger Venning*

No 1338 in the coaling queue at Taunton shed, May 1947. A gas tank wagon for gassing coaches can just be seen to the left. *Roger Venning*

0-4-2T No 5812 was principally used as the West End carriage shunter, but was sometimes pressed into service on Chard branch passenger trains.

During World War Two, to keep Southern Railway men familiar with an alternative route in case their own was temporarily closed by enemy action, an SR crew, normally manning a T9 class 4-4-0, worked the 10.15am Exeter St David's to Taunton, the 2.05pm Taunton to Yeovil, returned with the 4.50pm Yeovil to Taunton, and made its way back to home territory with the 6.20pm Taunton to Exeter. The T9s were not strong engines and required rear end assistance from Wellington to Whiteball if the load exceeded four coaches. One GWR driver at Taunton said that they were 'lovely engines' and he liked the steam reverser which he considered was much better than that fitted to the GWR 'Aberdares'. If a T9's tender was filled with water from the Yeovil Pen Mill supply, the engine would prime. When the Southern Region eventually took over Pen Mill, they issued pink tablets to crews, and when a tank was filled, a tablet, nicknamed an 'aspirin', was popped in. It caused the water in the gauge glass to turn black.

SR 'Remembrance' class N15X 4-6-0s, on loan to the GWR from late 1941 until mid-1943, appeared at Taunton and among other duties worked the Exeter to Swindon goods. They were not popular, for with more than 16 wagons they needed assistance up Wellington Bank. After Nationalisation, ex-SR engines appeared regularly on trains from Barnstaple – mostly U class 2-6-0s and M7 0-4-4Ts.

In March 1944 Taunton was allocated brand-new LM class 8F 2-8-0s Nos 8433 and 8434, built at Swindo by the GWR. These were moved by early 1946 whe No 8440 of the same type arrived, this staying until Ap 1947. On these engines an Automatic Train Contr ramp at Caution opened a small capacity cylinder of th vacuum-operated steam brake valve, applying the stea brake immediately. This meant that when banking up Whiteball with an 8F in front as train engine, if an AT ramp was at Caution, the brakes were quickly applie the wagons went into the 8F and, unless quick action w taken, the banker went into the train with conseque risk of de-railing wagons. To avoid this problem, a larg vacuum cylinder was fitted.

Similar problems were experienced with LNER B class 4-6-0s which hauled ambulance trains over lines the Big Four during World War Two, an ATC ramp Caution causing the air brake to be applied sudden These trains carried wounded servicemen to and fro Musgrove Park Hospital, Taunton, built by th Americans. The casualties were unloaded at the passeng station. B12s went to Taunton shed for the clinker to raked out, leaving three-quarters of an hour later. Th coaches were taken to Blinkhorn Sidings where they wer cleaned and their medical and food supplies replenishe for the return journey, usually to Southampton.

Ex-LMS 'Jubilee' class 4-6-0s occasionally appeared Taunton from 1961 running from Bristol to Taunto with a passenger train if no other engine was availabl No 45660 *Rooke* being recorded on such a turn.

London & North Eastern Railway A1 class pacific No 4474 *Victor Wild* at Taunton in 1925, during the Locomotive Exchange Trials. *J F King Collection*

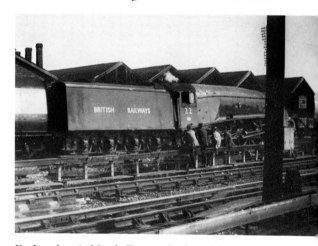

Ex-London & North Eastern Railway No 22 *Mallard* leavin Taunton with the 8.30am Plymouth to Paddington expres during the 1948 Locomotive Exchanges. *Tony Harve*

The sidings of the Permanent Way Depot and Concrete Works on the Up side at the east end of Taunton passenger station were worked by No 24, a four-wheel 40 bhp petrol-mechanical Simplex with chain drive. Built in 1926 it was scrapped in 1960. It was driven by permanent way staff who were not qualified to drive outside the depot. It was a very unreliable machine and often a steam locomotive had to be supplied as a

substitute worked by a Taunton shed crew. The driver No 24 collected petrol from the hand-worked pum across the goods depot normally used for filling lorrie He filled 12 to 15 two-gallon cans and pushed them bac on a two-wheeled hand cart. Sister machine No 23, buil in 1925 and scrapped in 1960, and which acquired a cab roof mounted warning bell, was equally unreliable. It wa used on the Docks branch at Bridgwater.

Southern Railway Plymouth Friary to Waterloo express at platform 6 on 8th September 1946. This train was diverted via Dulverton due to floods at Hele & Bradninch and a landslip near Honiton. Double-headed by T9 class 4-4-0 No 731 and N class 2-6-0 No 1875, it regained home metals at Yeovil.   *Roger Venning*

A fast freight to Tavistock Junction yard, Plymouth, hauled by LMS 8F No 8438 (Old Oak Common), pauses at Fairwater Bridge, 7th December 1946.
Roger Venning

Petrol shunter No 24 at Taunton concrete depot, c.1950. The Simplex builder's plate is on the dash.

Author's Collectio

It is said that the first BR Standard Class 9F 2-10-0 to be used on a passenger train worked from Taunton. Nothing else being available, the 9F was pressed into service and kept time. Other sheds heard of this use and so these engines became quite widely used on passenger duties.

Some Taunton engines were out-shedded – such as a 22XX or 55XX stabled at Minehead overnight to work the first Up passenger train the next morning. Similarly a 22XX or 43XX worked the first Up train from Barnstaple. Yeovil branch duties were shared between Taunton and Yeovil men. No engines were left overnight on the Chard branch, but three locomotives were shedded overnight for a week at Bridgwater, these generally being ex-Cardiff Railway No 1338 and 4-wheeled petrol shunter No 23 for working the Docks, and one of the 2021 class 0-6-0PTs for West End shunting. Three pairs of men were stationed at Bridgwater to crew these engines.

At maximum, around 1947, 144 crews were based at Taunton shed. About this period there was such a shortage of staff that within a few weeks of being appointed cleaner, a boy would be out firing on a shunting tank engine. Drivers and firemen were paired, remaining together until either one was promoted to a higher link, or one was on a 'spare shift' – that is, no

designated job, but used to cover other jobs lackin manning due to holidays or sickness. Drivers an firemen were allocated to 'links' where there might be 2 or more jobs and when they had covered the cycle ove that number of weeks, started again.

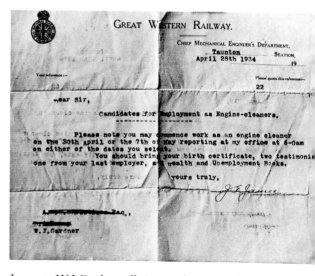

Letter to W J Gardner offering employment as Engine Cleaner.

A South Wales to Hackney yard, Newton Abbot, fast freight, hauled by No 6873 *Caradoc Grange*, leaves Taunton East yard via the goods loop. The permanent way depot buildings can be seen in the left background, February 1947. *Roger Venning*

The bottom link was the Local Yard Shunters (including the Preparation Link) covering 24-hour working at the Up and Down side yards at the east end of the station, and the West yard and Fairwater Sidings at the west end of the station. Further progress of a driver was to the Chard and Minehead Link to cover any positions that were not taken over by older drivers who for health reasons had been removed from main line duties; then to No 4 Link covering other branch freight and passenger trains and quite a few depot relief jobs where they could be shifted up to two hours either side of designated booking-on time in order to cover other men on holiday or sick. Such turns were disliked, because crew did not know, until the job sheet was studied, what time they were required to book on, and this uncertainty could affect their social life.

The next move was to No 3 Link operating branch freight and passenger trains and main line local freight such as to Highbridge and Tiverton Junction, but chiefly responsible for main line freight trains on a 'Control Relief' basis whereby after booking on, both driver and fireman reported by phone to Exeter Train Control Office to await orders as to which footplate crew required relief. Destinations for this link could be Exeter, Newton Abbot or Bristol where the train might terminate or another set of men relieve them.

No 2 Link covered most of the main line fast freight. In 1960 the link worked such trains as:

(a) The Hackney yard to Cardiff freight, 2.30am ex-Taunton, Taunton men working the 'Hall' or 'Grange' through to Cardiff and returning with the 7.50pm Cardiff to Newton Abbot with a 'Hall', 'Grange' or Class 9F. On arrival at Taunton, another Taunton crew took it on to its destination.

(b) The 4.15am Fairwater yard to Banbury D class freight, the crew working a Taunton 'Hall' to Swindon.

(c) The 1.55pm Taunton to Bristol stopping passenger with a 'Hall', 'Castle' or 9F, returning with the same locomotive on the 6.15pm Bristol West depot to Taunton East yard.

(d) The 2.50pm ex-Penzance (12.17am Taunton – it stopped at every station) to Paddington C class freight with a Plymouth 'Hall', the Taunton crew working from Taunton to Westbury.

(e) The 4.35pm passenger to Barnstaple with a 63XX returning with the 8.15pm freight to Bristol. The locomotive was changed at Taunton for a 'Hall' or 'Grange' with another Taunton crew.

(f) The 9.30pm Fairwater yard to Acton D class freight as far as Newbury with a Taunton 'Hall', or ex-LMS 8F of the balanced type marked by a white star on the cab. These were allowed to do 50 mph instead of the 40 mph to which the 'unbalanced' 8Fs were limited. The crew returned with the 10.10pm Paddington to Plymouth freight.

The top link worked most of the local main line passenger trains such as the 6.35, 7.02 and 7.50am to Bristol; the 7.20am Exeter North Mail to Plymouth return, with the Up 'Royal Duchy', being relieved by Taunton men to Paddington, returning in later years with the 12.30am Paddington to Plymouth C headcode freight. At various periods Taunton men worked the 6.30am Plymouth to Paddington, returning with the Down 'Royal Duchy'; and the Up 'Flying Dutchman', returning with the Down 3.30pm ex-Paddington.

The East & West Carriage Shunting Link engines were generally manned by drivers whose health precluded them from driving on main, or branch lines. They were paired with young firemen and this link had no night turns; in fact it was just one early and one late shift at each end of the station, making a total of four turns.

On Sunday mornings, Taunton depot staff firemen awaiting advancement attended Mutual Improvement Classes in order to increase each other's knowledge of the job, both of the theory and practice of steam locomotive working. Attendance at these proved *very* important when firemen were interviewed at Swindon for upgrading.

Drivers were only allowed to work trains over lines for which they had signed for route knowledge, being given the opportunity to ride in company time on the footplate with another competent driver in order to learn the road; this entailed being aware of the position of signals and signalboxes, gradients, positions of catch points and crossovers; and on single lines, the method of working, whether it be by the Electric Train Staff or Tablet; Staff and Tickets; and/or One Engine in Steam.

Most crews considered that booking on after 8.00pm or before 6.00am, for the night or early turns, were the ones they most disliked.

Poor steaming of a locomotive could be affected by various things, the main causes being dirty tubes or tubeplate, poor quality coal, or leaking steam pipes. The best coal was Welsh Steam from such collieries as Abergorki, Great Western engines being designed to burn this type of coal in a Belpaire firebox. Welsh coal had a high fixed carbon content and did not generate large volumes of smoke as did coal from some of the Midland collieries such as Blidworth. Welsh coal also had a very high calorific value being as high in some cases as 18,000 to 19,000 BTUs/lb, whereas a hard type of coal could be as low as 11,000 BTUs/lb. Using such a lower grade of fuel required careful management of the fire, especially in view of the fact that it also fused together to make a lot of clinker which severely restricted the primary supply of air entering through the dampers to pass through the fire bars to the bed of the fire. Provided that the tubes, tubeplate and smokebox steam pipe joints were clear and not blowing, most engines would maintain steam pressure very well until the fire bed started to clinker, when the only cure was to put the engine on shed and have the fire cleaned. Fire-dropping, tube-cleaning, fire-lighting and boiler-washing duties were carried out by the shed labouring staff.

Taunton Mutual Improvement Class pose in front of the graceful Dean Single No 3039 *Dreadnought*, c.1910. Part of steam Railmotor No 69 can be seen on the left.
J F King Collection

No 5973 *Rolleston Hall* (Reading) hauls a Down goods through platform 1 of the passenger station on 7th October 1946. This was unusual as normally on weekdays, freight trains used the goods loop. A sign warns staff using the walkway at the platform ends to 'Stop. Look. Listen'.
Roger Venning

No 2876 (Newport, Ebbw Junction) drops off wagons at the East yard before proceeding to Riverside yard, Exeter in March 1947. A shunter, armed with his pole, crosses an adjacent line.
Roger Venning

Firemen on the GWR were expected to prepare the engine while their drivers 'oiled-up' and carried out an examination of the locomotive. Preparation consisted of examining the pipework, spark arrester plate and blast pipe jumper ring to test security and freedom; checking the cleanliness of the tubes; sweeping all excess smokebox ash from the front footplate; checking sanding-gear operation and sand box levels; fitting front and tail lamps and then attending to the fire in order to have the water level and steam pressure ready so that the engine could perform its duties at the required time.

Quite a wide range of repairs was carried out at Taunton shed:

(a) The removal of valves and pistons for the purpose of dislodging carbon deposits on valves, pistons and in the steam chests and cylinders. If this had been allowed to build up it would have caused loss of efficiency due to the rings sticking.
(b) Changing worn brake blocks.
(c) Changing main springs if a broken leaf was found by a driver preparing his engine.
(d) Packing steam chest and piston glands. (Firemen were expected to re-pack valve glands on all slide valve engines, eg 57XX 0-6-0PTs and 22XX 0-6-0s).
(e) Re-packing of various leaking joints.

(f) Replacement of defective boiler and superheater tubes.
(g) The lifting shop was equipped with a large hoist suitable for lifting any class of engine for such tasks as the removal of axle boxes where the whitemetal lining had overheated and run. Axle box white metalling was normally replaced at Swindon works and returned for fitting at Taunton.
(h) Replacement of worn big ends, coupling rods and crosshead bushings.
(i) Dismantling and re-fitting of valve gear after checking, or replacing worn bushes.

During the last couple of years of World War Two an Italian prisoner-of-war worked at the locomotive shed shovelling ashes from the ground into railway wagons. At night he was confined to the Army Barracks at Taunton. So much did he enjoy the life that when peace was declared, he remained in Taunton and continued to shovel ashes for the GWR.

To celebrate the end of the war with the Axis powers, on 8th May 1945 a small group of loco spotters was enthralled when 2-6-0 No 6364 started running up and down on the shed roads exploding detonators. This was encored by 0-4-2T No 5812, the West End shunter exploding detonators laid on the track of bay platform 8

Smoke box ash being removed from 'Star' class No 4026 (named *The Japanese Monarch* until January 1941), at Taunton shed in 1947
Roger Venning

No 2665 (Oxley) with coupling rods and centre driving wheels removed. Replacement parts, wrapped in sacking, await fitting. In his 17th December 1946 view, No 2665 has an ex-ROD tender. To the right is Taunton 'Star' No 4056 *Princess Margaret*.

Roger Venning

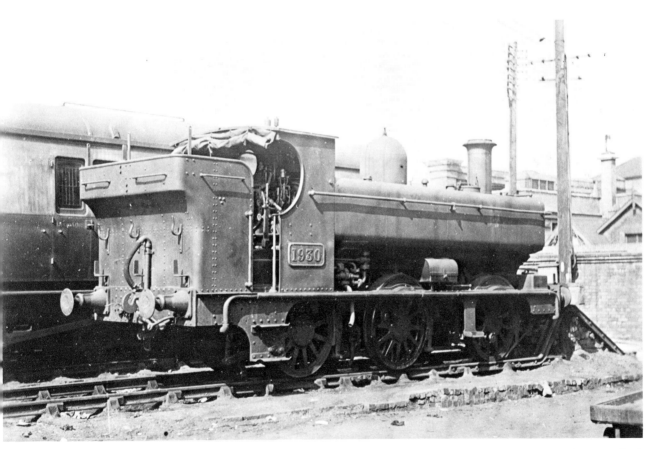

No 1930 (St Blazey), minus coupling rods, outside Taunton locomotive repair shed in the summer of 1939. Notice there is no back to the cab, a tarpaulin being provided to hook on to three uprights in inclement weather.

Bob Franklin

No 3202 stands in the shed road. The corrugated building right, is the repair shop. Notice the Loco Carriage & Wagon Department tool van left.
S P Bowditch Collection

No 7337 and an unidentified 'Hall' stand near the repair shop, while a diesel shunts coaches in platform 3.   *Lens of Sutton*

Official inspection of the new locomotive round-house in its pristine glory before its opening in 1896. Mr Christie, Locomotive Divisional Superintendent, stands on the centre of the plank across one of the pits.
J F King Collection

0-4-2T No 1450 stands beside a diesel shunter in the shed, May 1964.

Phil Cox

The Big Freeze of 1947 had a considerable effect on train working. Main line trains were so late arriving at Taunton that the last passenger train to Chard, instead of leaving on schedule at 8.55pm, most evenings had to wait for connections until close on midnight. A fireman on the morning goods to Minehead remembers that he had to turn the 22XX class 0-6-0 as soon as it arrived in order to shelter from the freezing east wind blowing from Dunster. Each pit in Taunton engine shed had a large steel brazier with a blazing fire to keep the water feed pipes between engine and tender and the feed injectors themselves from freezing. Depot relief drivers and firemen were kept busy maintaining these fires and ensuring that the injectors were in working order by periodically operating them for short intervals. In addition, spare firemen or engine cleaners were pressed into service day and night to keep the fires alight in other braziers located at each water column in the station and yards, coal being transported in wheelbarrows from the loco yard. Another onerous duty was freeing coal frozen in wagons at the coal stage so that engine tenders and bunkers could be replenished as they passed under the coal tip. The coal was loosened with whatever tools were at hand – such as steel bars and coal picks.

No 6016 *King Edward V* (Plymouth, Laira) heads a Penzance to Paddington express in late January 1947.   *Roger Venning*

No 6007 *King William III* (Old Oak Common) with the 8.30am Plymouth to Paddington express in late January 1947. *Roger Venning*

In late January 1947, due to points icing up, this Taunton to Bristol train had to start from Down main platform 5. Being an Up train, such a departure was highly unusual. Locomotive No 6965 (Swindon) is un-named, but later became *Thirlestaine Hall*.

Roger Venning

No 2212 (Taunton) nears the end of its journey with a Minehead to Taunton passenger train on 29th January 1947. *Clive Bousfield*

No 7809 *Childrey Manor* (Bristol, Bath Road) at platform 7 with a stopping train to Bristol, January 1947.

Roger Venning

No 4117 (Taunton) with tablet exchanger fitted next to the numberplate at Fairwater yard on 5th January 1947, a bitterly cold winter's day. The cab shutter has been slid over to give maximum protection to the crew.
Roger Venning

Men of the Outdoor Department at Taunton shed who maintained such items as water columns, enjoyed going to Bridgwater for the day to pack the glands and carry out basic maintenance of the dock's scraper-dredger *Bertha*. Away from the eyes of the foreman, they quickly carried out the necessary work and spent the rest of the day playing cards inside *Bertha*. The story runs that they looked up from their play one day and were surprised at the slope of the deck. Investigating, they discovered that the tide had fallen and the warps were not long enough to let *Bertha* sink to the water level.

From time to time amusing episodes occurred to Taunton footplate crews. On morning shifts it was the practice to fry eggs and bacon on a shovel, but it was fraught with danger because if the driver forgot that breakfast was being cooked and opened the steam ejector in order to release the brakes, eggs and bacon were likely to be swept to the top of the firebrick arch, leaving two hungry men blaming each other.

One driver of the Chard goods, when standing in the loop at Ilminster, used to think it hilarious to turn the boiler feed on and then spray the engine crew of the incoming passenger train with the coal slaking hose.

Taunton men were once about to move a United States Army Transportation Corps 2-8-0 onto the turntable from one of the long radial roads. It had been stabled next to the stationary boiler used for boiler washing and, being a pleasantly warm spot, the boiler washer and his mate had their supper sitting cosily by the stationary boiler's fire. Suddenly this tranquil scene was disturbed by steam lifting the 2-8-0's safety valves. They were set at an angle, instead of vertical as on most British engines, so that the steam hit the roof to right and left of the engine. The jets of steam blew the accumulated soot from the roof down, some landing on their sandwiches and in their tea mugs. They were not amused, but both would have qualified for a Minstrel show!

Taunton shed sometimes dealt with special trains. In 1958, Bob Chudleigh, fireman in No 3 Link, was the first to work a Sunday special to Weymouth, stopping at Athelney and the eleven stations to Yeovil Pen Mill. From there it ran non-stop to Weymouth, except for a halt at Evershot for rear banking assistance by an 0-6-0PT from Yeovil shed. It had been intended that 2-6-2T No 6113 should have had eight coaches, but such was the number of bookings that the load was strengthened to ten. On arrival at Weymouth the crew booked off duty on what was termed a 'Short Rest' and then booked on again in the evening about six hours later. An 0-6-0PT from Weymouth shed gave rear end assistance for the 1 in 50 climb to Bincombe Tunnel. It was a most successful day as the train was packed to standing.

American-built 2-8-0 No 2131 (Old Oak Common) hauls a down goods near Bradford-on-Tone, 27th August 1944. *Pursey Short*

A Paddington to Penzance express, hauled by No 6027 *King Richard I* (Newton Abbot), passes below Fairwater Bridge in mid-September 1947.

Roger Venning

Mixed traffic 2-8-0 No 4703, in unlined green livery, heads a passenger train on the Down relief line, 2nd September 1961.

John Cornelius

0-6-0 No 2266 at platform 7 with a Taunton to Yeovil train, c.1932. The photograph was taken in the summer as the engine has its steam heating pipe removed.
E J M Hayward

No 6025 *King Henry III*, with an Up stopping train to Bristol (despite express headlights), c.1932, soon after the station was rebuilt. The train is composed almost entirely of clerestory coaches. *E J M Hayward*

An Up train at platform 7, c.1932, headed by 2-6-0 No 6305 and No 4045 *Princess Charlotte*. As both engines carry 'B' class headlamps, it probably ran as a stopping train to Weston-super-Mare and then onwards as an express. *E J M Hayward*

Around 1958 various local factories were canvassed and special trains run to Wembley carrying audiences for pantomimes on ice. Taunton enginemen worked a Taunton locomotive throughout, stopping at Acton to pick up an Eastern Region pilot for the last few miles to Wembley. For this final part of the trip, in order to clear the electrified rail the Automatic Train Control shoe had to be clipped up out of use. The WR engine was stabled at Neasden depot until required to work the return journey.

In later years, during the summer months, specials were run to various resorts, a different one each day of the week and a mystery tour, as only the enginemen and guard knew the day's destination such as Dawlish, Teignmouth, Torquay & Paignton, Exmouth or Plymouth. These trains were well-patronised and enabled holidaymakers to sleep in their own beds at night.

On one occasion in 1957 Bob Chudleigh and his driver relieved an Oxford crew at Taunton. The train, hauled by No 7907 *Hart Hall*, consisted of coaches carrying Territorials to their summer camp at Tregantle Fort, Whitsand Bay, Cornwall – the first time in living memory that a Taunton crew had crossed the Saltash Bridge. As they only knew the road as far as Keyham, they stopped by Laira shed to pick up a pilotman to guide them to St Germans, the nearest station to the fort. A Plymouth crew brought out 'Castle' No 7000 *Viscount Portal*, tender-first, for the return journey, taking the empty stock back to Taunton and the pilotman back to Laira.

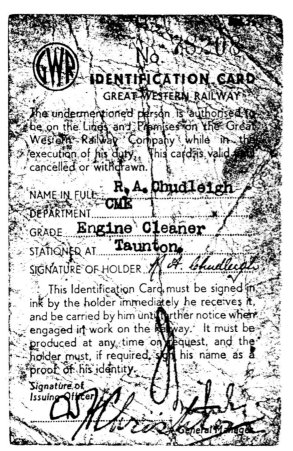

A special train worked by 63XX class 2-6-0 once carried Prince Philip to Dunster. A wagon of best Welsh coal was delivered to Taunton depot especially for this trip, the excess coal tipped on other engines following on down the coal road. One of these was 2-6-2T No 5571 which Bob Chudleigh fired the following day on a Bampton cattle special. He remembers vividly that she steamed so well that there was no need to close either the firehole doors or continually open and close the flap plate, and when he returned to shed, the fire was almost as clean as when he started that morning.

Before the Queen travelled to Barnstaple on 8th May 1956, the royal train was stabled overnight on the short branch line between Durston and Athelney. The following morning it was hauled to Barnstaple by 2-6-0 locomotive No 6372 of Taunton shed and No 6385 stabled at Exeter. Instead of being in the BR black livery they were painted green and fully lined out, with the safety valve covers polished. That autumn it became the official policy to repaint all the class unlined green and the following February, full lining was added.

Engines of the 'Castle' class were allowed on the Minehead branch as far as Bishops Lydeard, but it is believed the only one to take up this option was at the head of a royal train parked overnight.

It was not unusual for a guard to make an incorrect estimate of the weight of his train. One such occasion was when Bob Chudleigh and his driver were working the 9.30pm fast freight from Cardiff to Plymouth in 1956 behind No 4942 *Maindy Hall* and were wrongly informed of the load. They set out and made a very fast descent into the Severn Tunnel and although slowing appreciably, did not stop beyond at Pilning for a banker to give assistance up the three miles of 1 in 100, believing that the train load was within the capability of their engine. Part way up the incline, *Maindy Hall* started to struggle and only just managed with full regulator and maximum cut-off to reach the level track beyond Patchway Tunnel. The train continued non-stop through Temple Meads passenger station to Bridgwater where Bob's driver, still furious, berated the guard over the train's weight. He found it to be 85 tons over the limit of 420 tons for a 'Hall' on this route.

One night, 25 minutes before booking off time, a fireman in the Preparation and Yard Shunters Link decided that there would be no more work that night and that he could slip home early. Hardly had he gone out of sight when the driver received a call to pilot a train to Whiteball. There was really only one thing to do. To cover for the absent footplateman he had to fire and drive.

The 4-6-0 'Counties' were liked by Taunton men as they were economical engines. 'Counties' needed a bright, shallow fire like that of a 'Dean Goods' with which Taunton crews were very familiar, and they believed that Bristol men generally would not adapt themselves to the method of firing they required. 'County' dampers opened the opposite way to those of other GWR engines and not all firemen were aware of this, often blaming the engine for poor steaming, instead

AREA No. 5

SOMERSET and DEVON. No. 5.
17s. 6d. 3rd Class.

NOTE—Holiday Run-about Tickets are not available by the "Cornish Riviera" and "Torbay" Expresses during the period 11th June to 16th September inclusive.

SOMERSET and DEVON. No. 6. 17s. 6d. 3rd Class.

Tickets are also issued including trips on Messrs. P. & A. Campbell's Bristol Channel Steamers from Weston-super-Mare to Cardiff (Pierhead). Combined charge 25s., 3rd Class.
(Area No. 6A)

Passengers should enquire at stations for information regarding dates and times of steamer sailings, weather and circumstances permitting.

AREA No. 6

Travel by the "SOMERSET HOLIDAY EXPRESS"

CAFETERIA CAR TRAIN FROM BRIDGWATER, TAUNTON OR WELLINGTON TO DIFFERENT RESORTS EACH DAY

(6th August to 10th August inclusive)

MONDAY, 6th AUGUST	EXMOUTH
TUESDAY, 7th AUGUST	PLYMOUTH
WEDNESDAY, 8th AUGUST	TEIGNMOUTH
THURSDAY, 9th AUGUST	CLIFTON DOWN
FRIDAY, 10th AUGUST	WEYMOUTH

5 DAYS' TRAVEL FOR

51/6 from BRIDGWATER   **45/6** from TAUNTON
44/6 from WELLINGTON

Your Seat reserved free each day. For full details of train times, etc., see separate announcements.

Great Western Railway
CHEAP TRAVEL FACILITIES

To visit The Most Laughable, Spectacular and Beautifully Dressed of all Pantomimes

ALADDIN

at

Knightstone Theatre
WESTON-SUPER-MARE

Commencing Monday, Dec. 23rd at 6.45
Times of Performances MON. TUES. & WEDS 2.15 & 6.45
THURS. & FRI. 2.15 & 8.0 SATURDAYS at 2.0, 5.0 & 8.15

Terminating Saturday, January 18th.

Week Commencing Monday, Jan. 20th.
THE ROYAL IMPERIAL CIRCUS
MATINEES Tues. Wed. & Thurs. at 2.30.   Nightly at 7.30
Saturday 2.30 5.15 & 8.0

(Same Railway Facilities)

Each Tuesday, Wednesday and Thursday cheap Day Tickets

to

WESTON-S-MARE

Available in Each Direction by any Train the same Day

From	RETURN FARES			
	First Class		Third Class	
	s.	d.	s.	d.
TAUNTON	7	11	5	9
BRIDGWATER	4	7	2	9
HIGHBRIDGE	2	8	1	8

Convenient Forward Trains							Convenient Return Trains				
	a.m.	a.m.	p.m.	p.m.	p.m.	p.m.		p.m.	p.m.	p.m.	p.m.
Taunton Dep.	10.15	11.35	1.20	2.25	4.35	5.8	Weston-s-M Dep.	4.55	6.35	8.22	10.0
Bridgwater Dep.	10.36	11.55	1.42	2.46	5.0	5.30	Highbridge Arr.	5.17	6.58	8.42	10.17
Highbridge Dep.	10.50	12.13	1.57	3.0	5.15	5.45	Bridgwater Arr.	5.32	7.17	8.55	10.26
Weston-s-M Arr.	11.9	12.31	2.52	3.28	5.36	6.3	Taunton Arr.	5.55	7.40	9.20	10.45

B. & M. Organ, Theatrical Printers, Wrington, Somerset.

WESTERN **BRITISH RAILWAYS** REGION

DAILY
(WHERE TRAIN SERVICE PERMITS)
JUNE 1st and UNTIL FURTHER NOTICE

"SUMMERTIME"
CHEAP TICKETS
WILL BE ISSUED AS ENUMERATED HEREIN FROM

STATIONS IN THE
EXETER, TAUNTON & TORBAY AREAS

AVAILABLE FOR USE

By Any Train after 9.30 a.m.

PROVIDED THE RETURN JOURNEY IS COMMENCED THE SAME DAY AS THE OUTWARD JOURNEY.

Break of journey is not allowed, but passengers holding these tickets are allowed to alight at a station short of destination in either direction on surrender of ticket and to return from any intermediate station.

SPECIAL NOTE—Cheap Tickets issued from Exeter to Newton Abbot, Torre, Torquay and Paignton will be available for return by the 1.0 a.m. (night) train from Newton Abbot and the connecting service from the Kingswear Branch which leaves Paignton at 12.5 a.m., Torquay 12.12 a.m. and Torre 12.19 a.m. arriving Exeter (St. David's) 1.30 a.m.
(TRAIN SERVICE SUBJECT TO ALTERATION)

FIRST CLASS TICKETS AT APPROXIMATELY 50 PER CENT. OVER THE THIRD CLASS FARE WILL ALSO BE ISSUED WHERE FIRST CLASS ACCOMMODATION IS AVAILABLE.

Children under Three years of age, Free ; Three and under Fourteen years of age, half-fare.
NOTICE AS TO CONDITIONS.—These tickets are issued subject to the Conditions of Issue of Ordinary passenger tickets, where applicable, and also to the special Conditions as set out in the Ticket, etc., Regulations, Bye-Laws, and General Notices. Luggage allowances are as set out in these General Notices.

Tickets can be obtained in advance at Booking Stations and Agencies.

Further information will be supplied on application to Booking Stations, Agencies, or to Mr. D. H. HAWKESWOOD, District Commercial Superintendent, Exeter (St. David's) (Telephone Exeter 2281, Extension 301, 302 or 303) ; or to Mr. C. FURBER, Commercial Superintendent, Paddington Station, W.2.

Paddington Station, W.2.
April, 1953

K. W. C. GRAND,
Chief Regional Officer.

109

of themselves. Jack Gardner once fired No 1013 *County of Dorset* heading the Up sleeper loaded to 13 coaches. This engine certainly proved economical and only used about half a tank of water between Taunton and Reading where they thought it wisest to stop as the water pick-up was not functioning.

An example of local working is as follows. A Taunton crew booking on at 4.00am would take 0-6-0PT No 5412 on the 5.05am to Bridgwater and back, propelling the auto coaches in the outward direction. Then they worked the 6.05am to the same destination and back, on through Taunton to Venn Cross and returned to Taunton. Then they worked the 8.48am to Castle Cary and back, returning to shed about 11.30am where the engine shunted coal wagons. An interesting point about auto working was that on occasions when the driver was in the control vestibule, if Rule 55 had to be carried out, which involved one of the crew going to the nearest signalbox, this was the guard's duty and not the fireman's as the latter had to remain on the footplate.

One porter at Wellington used to go all out to receive large tips. He had an eye for spotting rich old ladies whom he helped into a first class compartment; he carried their luggage in, held out his hand and was suitably rewarded. After tolerating this behaviour for a period, his colleagues thought it was time he was taught a lesson. One day the opportune moment arrived. The leading porter and the guard had a quiet word together and when the porter climbed aboard the train with the passenger's luggage, the guard blew the whistle before he could get out.

As the train left, his mates on the platform saw him gesticulating. 'It's all right,' they called, 'we'll have the train stopped at Whiteball'. They kept their word and the porter cadged a lift on the footplate of a returning banker. The driver, in on the joke, opened the regulator wide. The engine roared through the tunnel at about 70 mph, rocking and swaying and frightening the porter to death … but they had not finished with him yet. The driver now feigned a heart attack and collapsed.

The porter, surprised that the fireman did not take over the controls, yelled 'Can't you stop it?' 'No,' he replied, 'I only came on the job last week. I don't know what to do.'

The terrified porter, white with fear, climbed down the cab steps and was prepared to leap off the rapidly-moving engine. Only then was it revealed that it was a joke. The ploy certainly worked and he never purposely sought large tips again.

View from Forty Steps footbridge in the 1950s. Left to right: No 7014 *Caerhays Castle* with a Down express; No 4073 *Caerphilly Castle* heading a Down express freight; while No 2213 has a branch train for Minehead or Barnstaple.

Great Western Society, Taunton Group

Locomotive Sheds

The first shed at Taunton was a small two-road temporary timber building first erected at Bridgwater, then dismantled and re-erected at Taunton when the line was extended there in 1842. In 1860 this building was re-sited yet again, this time 120 feet east, nearer the passenger station in order to permit track alterations. This shed was eventually closed in April 1896 and replaced at a cost of £10,500 by a brick-built shed with a north-light pattern roof. The adjacent coal stage, of contemporary design, had a 35,000 gallon water tank above and coal wagons approached it up a ramp. The shed had 28 radiating roads. It held 26 engines, one on each line, one road being ingoing and another outgoing. The roof was supported by four pillars with seven bays between each. The longest road was too short to hold a 'King'. The shed's interior was very dark – too dark to take photographs, or sometimes even to see locomotives' numbers. A wedge-shaped snow plough was kept at the shed and attached to the front of a locomotive when required. From early years, if not initially, the turntable was worked by electric power. This power table was occasionally maltreated, some operators finding it easier to reverse the direction of movement to halt it, instead of using the footbrake. This abuse would cause a fuse to blow and as the electrician did not wish to be called out and paid for just five minutes work, he checked all the fuses from Obridge, east of the station, to the West sidings, before going to the shed. To avoid this expense, the table was converted to hand turning around 1936.

In 1932 a repair shop, of standard design and constructed with corrugated asbestos, was built between the shed and No 4 bay platform, and still stands though the main engine shed has long been demolished. Closed to steam in October 1964, the repair shop continued in use, but from 1st January 1972 fuelling facilities were withdrawn and servicing of main line locomotives and dmus discontinued. Drivers continued to book on at Taunton until 9th May 1986 after which the only crews boarding locomotives at the station were from other depots working home.

No 6398 (Taunton) with a freight from Barnstaple on the goods loop, 31st October 1946. It will terminate in the East yard sidings. Notice the coaling stage behind the engine.
Roger Venning

No 5039 *Rhuddlan Castle* (Old Oak Common), converted for oil-burning, leaves Taunton shed in July 1947.

Roger Venning

No 2215 (Taunton), with an ex-ROD tender, leaves the shed and joins the goods loop, 7th December 1946. The water tank and coal stage form a background.
Roger Venning

Oil-burning No 39..
Garth Hall (Bristol, Ba...
Road), has backed off sh...
before moving throu...
the station to couple to ...
stopping train to Bristol ...
platform 8, July 1947.

Roger Vennin...

Two rare visitors:
'Dukedog' No 3207
(Machynlleth) and No
3284 *Isle of Jersey*
(Stourbridge) in the
coaling queue, 2nd June
1946. *Roger Venning*

No 6002 *King William IV*
(Plymouth, Laira) in the
'dead engine' sidings with
a 'run' bearing. Left is
War Department 0-6-0ST
No 75165 and, right, WD
2-8-0 No 77077 (Taunton),
mid-August 1947.

Roger Venning

Water supply for locomotives and station purposes was taken from the Bridgwater & Taunton Canal. In January 1870 fire broke out just before 6.00am in the house containing the pump and although every effort was made to douse the flames, this proved impossible as the pickled timber burned so fiercely. A large watertank is still in existence at Firepool near the former goods shed. The water was formerly raised by a Stuart steam-driven pump, but later by one powered by electricity. Subsidiary tanks were sited over the coal stage, near the Signal & Telegraph Engineer's Department and at the West carriage sidings. The tank above the coal stage was raised in about 1906, the original level not giving a sufficiently good head of water. Around 1955 when a serious fire broke out at Easton & Johnson's Engineering Works in Albemarle Road near the goods loop, the local fire brigade was given access to the railway's supply as the town's relatively small bore pipes could not deliver enough water.

The shed's Outdoor Department maintained, among other things, the water pump at Williton on the Minehead branch. Although Minehead had a water supply, it came from the mains and, as this had to be paid for, the railway tried to avoid using it. Following Nationalisation, this department also took over the maintenance of the turntable at Ilfracombe. Fitted with 22 large ball bearings, each the size of a tennis ball, it was a good table, easy to turn and fitted with a footbrake. On one occasion, the wind caught an engine and kept it revolving, so smooth was its running, just as in the famous incident at Garsdale on the Settle & Carlisle.

The two-road timber shed at Bridgwater, opened in June 1841, was removed to Taunton 12 months later. The former town was then without a shed for many years until 1893 when a 120-ft long bay of the carriage works was adapted to stable the Carriage & Wagon shunter, and also that for working the Docks branch. As work in the shops declined, the other buildings were demolished, though the locomotive depot remained. A sub-shed of Taunton, it closed in July 1960.

The GWR, which was working the B&ER, provided a locomotive siding at Wellington in September 1844 for stabling and servicing the locomotive provided to assist trains up Wellington Bank, a small shed being erected the following May. It is not known when it closed, but it was still in use when the B&ER took over the working in 1849, yet no longer there when the B&ER was amalgamated with the GWR in 1876, as then the banking engines were supplied from Taunton.

No 3441 *Blackbird* (Plymouth, Laira) and No 1338 (Taunton, sub-shedded at Bridgwater) on the goods loop in April 1947. No 3441 is leaving the shed for the East yard to pick up a freight for Barnstaple.   *Roger Venning*

A Penzance to Manchester express about to leave platform 7 behind No 4037 *The South Wales Borderers* in 1938.

Interesting trips

In 1947, Taunton No 1 Link worked the North Mail to Plymouth, returning with the 2.00pm ex-Plymouth, except on Saturdays when they travelled home as passengers. On Saturday 26th July 1947, fireman Jack Gardner and driver Fred Mogg took their engine to shed at Laira where the shed foreman told them to travel home 'on the cushions'. They secured a lift to North Road station and were drinking a can of tea when a station inspector came up and asked if they were Taunton men. Receiving an affirmative reply, he said that the foreman had made a mistake and that they had 'back working' that day assisting the 11.05am Saturdays-only Par to Cardiff, loaded to 12 coaches.

They saw five light engines arrive coupled together: two were headed towards Cornwall, two towards the north, and the middle one was 'Bulldog' No 3383. Jack said to his mate Fred, 'I bet that's ours' and it was. When they boarded they found the engine was in a disgusting state – boiler lagging flapping like flags in a breeze and a tender full of small coal just like black gravel. They moved No 3383 to the engine siding by the Eye Hospital to await the train they were to assist.

Eventually it arrived headed by No 5065 *Newport Castle*, an engine which Jack and Fred had worked two weeks previously on the 5.05pm Paddington to Bristol and a very bad trip it had been. When they related this experience to its driver, his face fell as his regular fireman was not with him and he had a passed cleaner that day who would have had little, if any, experience of getting the utmost steam from a poor engine. They also told him that they had intended travelling back to Taunton on that very train but would not be able to because of having to take No 3383 to shed at Newton Abbot.

The driver of the 'Castle' made an agreement with Jack and Fred saying that if they assisted him well to Newton Abbot where Bristol men relieved him, he would come forward and take the engine to shed so that they could travel in that train.

The 11.05 ex-Par left Plymouth and they had only gone about three miles when Jack heard *Newport Castle's* blower on hard trying to make steam. They sailed through Plympton station 'at a good old pace' and on to Hemerdon Bank, nearly two miles of 1 in 42.

No 3383 was steaming well and maintaining full pressure with the exhaust injector on, though the smoke from its chimney could have been cut with a knife. A white house on the right-hand side gave a clear visual guide to footplate crews of their position on the bank and when Jack saw it, he thought he felt the train begin to lose momentum, so said to Fred 'We're OK, keep her going and drop the gear a notch further forward'. Fred replied, 'I can't, she's in full forward gear now!' No 3383 climbed the bank, regulator wide open, exhaust injector on and still maintaining pressure. Neither before nor after had Jack been on an engine which worked so hard.

Hemerdon and Dainton were eventually surmounted and *Newport Castle's* driver kept his word and took No 3383 to shed so that they were able to travel back to Taunton without having to wait for a later train.

Driver Harold Hunt and fireman Bob Chudleigh booked on at Taunton one Monday morning about 2.30am and took No 6815 *Frilford Grange* off shed to work forward a couple of eight-wheeled vans which had been detached from the Down newspaper train from Paddington. This arrangement permitted the main train to run non-stop from Taunton to Plymouth, the two vans putting off papers at Exeter, Teignmouth and Newton Abbot where the vans, now empty, were shunted into the carriage sidings. No 6815 then awaited the 11.50pm passenger ex-Paddington, nicknamed 'The Owl', which had travelled via Swindon, Bath and Bristol, rather than the more direct route via Castle Cary. 'The Owl', usually loaded to at least 13 or 14 coaches, required assistance up the Dainton and Rattery Inclines. On this occasion the 'Warship' class diesel-hydraulic heading the train arrived at Newton Abbot with one of its engines defective and shut down. The diesel driver had only just managed to haul his load on the flat and said that there was no way that the 'Grange' could take the crippled 'Warship' and train over Dainton. Harold Hunt took up this challenge and No 6815 gallantly worked up both inclines at 45 per cent cut off and full regulator which certainly roused the echoes passing Stoneycombe Sidings. On arrival at Plymouth, Messrs Hunt and Chudleigh received the diesel driver's congratulations. He said they did so well that he had not a moment's concern, but wondered how long they could keep up that tremendous effort. The secret was that the water sacrificed on the climbs was renewed on the descents. This ability to 'mortgage the boiler' was one of the great advantages of steam locomotives, enabling a skillful crew temporarily to get more out of an engine than it was normally capable of giving.

During the summer, especially on Saturdays, the passed firemen in the Taunton Passenger Link were given driving turns and therefore firemen in the lower links were pressed into service in their stead on Paddington or Plymouth passenger trains. On one such occasion in 1959, Bob Chudleigh found himself firing to his father, Reg Chudleigh. On this particular day, the 1.30pm Down was running in three parts – the first left Paddington at 1.20 with Dawlish its first stop. The second part of the express, with Bob firing, stopped at Reading and Taunton, leaving Paddington five minutes later. An Old Oak Common crew ran 'Castle' No 5056 *Earl of Powis* light to Paddington where it was coupled to 11 coaches. The 1.25 did not have a clear road to Reading as it was preceded by a Paddington to Weymouth train of about 12 coaches headed by a 63XX class Mogul – on busy summer Saturdays almost every engine was pressed into service even if it was not an ideal type for working a particular duty.

In consequence of this delay, Bob's train left Reading about nine minutes late but overtook the Weymouth

In June 1947, No 3408 *Bombay* (Didcot) pilots No 5016 *Montgomery Castle* (Swansea, Landore) on a Penzance to Manchester express. The train stands at platform 7. No 3408 was scrapped a year later. A wheel-tapper is at work.

Roger Venning

train at Newbury. Then his father set about recovering the lost minutes. *Earl of Powis* was steaming wonderfully well and Bob urged his father to keep going, even on the downhill run west of Savernake. From then on they were in the high eighties much of the way and ran into Taunton dead on time.

Bob vividly remembers another trip from Taunton to Paddington on No 6007 *King William III*. This engine had been removed from a Down train a few days previously with a hot axle box. Taunton shed had carried out repairs, and Bob and driver Bill Holcombe used it to take forward a passenger train from Minehead. Being towards the end of the summer season, it was only loaded to six coaches, or about 200 tons, and certainly was no problem for a 'King'. By the time Bob reached Savernake he had filled the firebox to such an extent that for the remaining 70 miles to Paddington, he did not put on any more than about 20 shovelfuls of coal and wished all trips could have been as easy.

Some Taunton men working to Paddington tried to stop shovelling coal as early as possible, one not putting any more into the firebox after Bedwyn, 61½ miles from Paddington. He was certainly taking a risk – had his engine been stopped by signals, he would have been short of steam. Normally, Reading was the place where one could stop firing with reasonable safety.

Another 'King' fired by Bob was No 6000 *King George V*. As it was a General Election day, in order to allow Old Oak Common men to return home to vote, they were relieved at Taunton instead of working a 'double-home' to Plymouth. (A double-home was a trip where you slept before returning.) Bob Chudleigh was very pleased to have the opportunity of firing *King George V*. She gleamed under the station lights as she ran in, for Old Oak Common men kept their passenger engines in very good condition. As the war had been over for about ten years, poor coal was not the order of the day and best Welsh coal was on the tender. The load was very manageable – about 11 vehicles totalling 330 tons. Only 58 minutes were allowed for the 50¾ miles to Newton Abbot and in view of the 40–50 mph speed restriction along the coast beyond Starcross, the crew were not sluggards between Taunton and Exminster because they wished to have sufficient time to observe the checks. All went well and no problems were encountered climbing Dainton and Rattery banks and the fire was let down ready for servicing on arrival at Laira shed. Bob was certain that the 'Kings' were masters of their job.

It was not quite the same story one day in 1959, by which time double-home workings had been abandoned allowing men to return to their own beds at night. At Taunton, Bob Chudleigh and his regular driver, Harold Hunt, relieved the Plymouth crew working the 8.30am Plymouth to Paddington express passenger due to leave Taunton at 10.47. On handing over, the Laira fireman told Bob that No 6003 *King George IV* was losing water at a phenomenally high rate and that he had not been able to discover the reason. Although he had filled

right up on Exminster Troughs, the tender was nearly empty on arrival at Taunton. They filled up before leaving and set off for Paddington. Maximum pressure was only 180 lbs instead of 250 lbs and they slowed down through Langport station, dropping off a message requesting assistance at Castle Cary. There, an 0-6-0PT was coupled inside the 'King' and they struggled on to Westbury with hardly any water in the gauge glass. The tank was filled yet again and a 'Hall' replaced the pannier tank engine. Eventually Paddington was reached 40 minutes late. A few weeks later Bob saw Inspector Vercoe of Western Region Headquarters at Newton Abbot who informed him that Old Oak Common had stripped down No 6003 after that journey and discovered the fault – a split firebox.

Another trip the same year involved taking the morning Taunton East yard to Plymouth (Tavistock Junction) goods train with No 2814, a Taunton 2-8-0, turning at Laira shed and returning light engine to Taunton. Having no load, they travelled at about 60 mph most of the way home and discovered on arrival at Taunton shed that liquid metal from a hot bearing had sprayed the underside of the boiler.

The fastest Bob ever travelled down Wellington Bank was on a 'King', reaching 98 mph. He also remembers achieving 89 mph near Westbury on a Taunton 'Bulldog' class No 3444 *Cormorant* piloting a 'King' hauling a Plymouth to Paddington express – and with only 5ft 8in driving wheels, that roughly equalled, in revolutions per minute, *City of Truro*'s achievement of 102.6 mph with 6ft 8½in driving wheels. 'Bulldogs' were smooth-riding engines and could travel fast without rocking like a 'Hall' or 'Saint'.

Taunton men worked trains to Ilfracombe with a 63XX class 2-6-0, the largest locomotive allowed over the branch. The steps of these engines were cut back to a width of 8ft 4in to give them sufficient clearance when working over the Southern Railway between Barnstaple and Ilfracombe. The maximum load for a 2-6-0 Taunton to Barnstaple was 10 coaches and the assistance of an SR engine was required up the gradient of 1 in 36 to Mortehoe. It was 123 miles to Ilfracombe and back to Taunton, and with 10 coaches and a 63XX this was quite hard going. The engine provided was usually fitted with a staff catcher which enabled it to run through intermediate stations without stopping, the only booked calls on the outward run being at Wiveliscombe, Dulverton, South Molton, Barnstaple Junction, and then all stations to Ilfracombe. The same stops were made on the return journey.

Following Nationalisation, occasionally an SR N class 2-6-0 would work through to Taunton. These were liked by WR drivers and, although rough to ride on, were considered 'strong' engines. T9 class 4-4-0s were also authorised and worked on a regular trip in 1953. Unrebuilt 'West Country' and 'Battle of Britain' pacifics could be used in an emergency, but were restricted to a limit of 20 mph, because of their weight.

Summer Saturday working in the late fifties could be

frustrating to both crews and passengers. When Bob booked on for duty with driver Jack Paddon on 27th July 1957 expecting a trip on the Barnstaple branch, they were surprised to find that they had been booked to relieve the crew of the 6.40am Leicester to Kingswear, seven coaches hauled by No 6997 *Bryn-Ivor Hall*. After leaving Taunton station, traffic was so heavy that they were stopped at every signal to Norton Fitzwarren, taking 40 minutes for the distance of two miles.

Instead of the scheduled 75 minutes to Newton Abbot, the journey took three and a half hours. They returned with the 5.30pm stopping train from Kingswear headed by No 7901 *Dodington Hall*, with nine coaches behind the tender. Stopping at all stations they returned in 2 hrs 16 mins.

One Sunday, around 1947, the 12.48pm Up express was composed of 17 coaches and at its head was 'Star' class No 4021 *British Monarch*, assisted to Savernake by No 6850 *Cleeve Grange*. *British Monarch* passed Reading on the through road and beyond overtook No 5032 *Usk Castle* with a load of only about six coaches. Its driver looked back to see the length of the train overtaking him and when he saw its weight, tried to accelerate, but did not succeed in catching *British Monarch*.

Driver Arthur Stockman was once returning from Yeovil with a passenger train and west of Cogload Junction opened the regulator down the slope beyond the flyover and overtook some of the coaches passing on the parallel Down main. A sailor on this express handed over a glass of beer as he overtook. Driver Stockman drank it, closed the regulator and let the main line train catch up, handing back the glass.

In 1938, the crew of No 4019 *Knight Templar* pose before leaving with a Down express. *Bob Franklin*

Accidents and Mishaps

e B&ER had a marvellous accident-free record and
med that it never killed a passenger. The broad gauge
s inherently very safe and what would have been a
aster on the standard gauge, was fatal only to the
tplate crew of a broad gauge train.

n instance of this was on 8th September 1852 when
9.45am express from Paddington was drawn from
stol by B&ER No 20, a 4-2-2 express tender engine
lt by Longridge & Co in 1849. The train consisted of
iron-built luggage van and two first, and two second-
ss coaches. According to one passenger, more coke
s loaded into the tender during the stop at Bridgwater.
m Durston there was a slight decline to the point
ere the line passed under the Chard Canal and then
e to Bathpool. It was usual practice for trains to go fast
fore this bridge in order to have no problem climbing
e incline beyond, but on this occasion, No 20
proached the bridge at an estimated 44 mph.

s the cutting on either side of the canal bridge was
rough clay, and surface water drained into this dip, for
yards the sides and base of the cutting were supported
substantial masonry termed an 'invert'.

fter No 20 had reached the Taunton side of the
vert, it became derailed and ran into the embankment.
he tender somersaulted and landed upside down on the
iler. The coupling chain behind the van broke as this
hicle was up-ended. Fortunately only the doors of the
ssing free-wheeling passenger coaches were damaged
this van before it fell back fouling the Up and Down
ads. The coaches stopped 150 yards beyond, just the
st coach being derailed. Only one passenger was
jured, suffering a slight cut on the face. The *Taunton*
urier reported:'It is said that, so unconscious [of the
cident] was one of the ladies in a first-class carriage,
at she said her attention was first attracted to it by
eing an engine pass rapidly in a contrary direction; this
ust have been the disabled engine, half buried in the
mbankment'.

The footplate crew were not so fortunate. The body
fireman Thomas Humberstone was seen protruding
om the earth. Shovels were obtained, and he was
ug out, dreadfully mutilated and burnt, and the
orpse removed to the Bell Inn, Creech St Michael, to
vait the coroner's inquest. Driver Lambert Eaton
uffered a crushed chest and a damaged left hand and,
ogether with travelling porter Joseph Tozer who
ad a broken leg, was taken to Taunton & Somerset
ospital, Eaton dying four days later. Guard Chivers
ll through the knocked-out end of his van into a pool
f water.

As the luggage van blocked both lines, Charles
ouracre, a ganger working nearby, went down the line
stop the Up express. The track was cleared by the
mple expedient of attaching the express engine to the
an and dragging it clear of the Up line, the express
ontinuing on its way two hours late.

The Board of Trade inspecting officer, Captain Robert
Michael Laffan, RE, unable to discover a definite cause
of the accident, believed that the axle of the leading set
of tender wheels was weak and broke on a rough section
of track. This caused the tender to derail and it struck
the rear of the engine when the leading wheels were on
a poor rail, with the result that the locomotive came off
the track. The permanent way was rough near the point
where the invert met the clay bed, due to water making
the clay wet and therefore unable adequately to support
the track.

James Pearson, B&ER locomotive superintendent,
expressed surprise that the axle was faulty, as the engine
was ex-works on 19th August, had hauled ballast trains for
a few days to get run in and then worked regular trains.

Sometimes railway servants suffered fatal injuries due
to their own carelessness. One such incident occurred on
29th July 1875 to Fred Stone, aged 22, a fireman who
lived at Barnstaple. The *Somerset County Gazette* of 7th
August reported the inquest:

Fatal Accident

*The coroner for this district (Mr Munckton) held an
enquiry on Saturday at Pane's, Golden Lion Inn, East
Reach into the circumstances attending the death of
Fred Stone, a single man, 22 years of age, who resided
at Barnstaple.*

*Inspector Green watched the proceedings on behalf of
the Bristol and Exeter Railway Co. Henry Frost,
engine driver, on the Bristol and Exeter Railway,
stated that on the previous Thursday he drove the
1/15pm train on the Devon & Somerset line from
Barnstaple, arriving at Milverton about 3 o'clock. The
train was rather late that day, and did not arrive at
Taunton until 3.38, being ten minutes behind time.*

*Soon after leaving Milverton, Stone said he had two
or three potatoes which he would put into the safety
valve of the engine to cook for his tea. He got on to the
boiler for that purpose, and immediately he (witness)
heard a blow on the watch board. They were passing
under the Pig & Whistle Bridge, in the parish of Oake
at the time.*

*He then saw Stone lying on the coal in the tender, and
having pulled him up, saw that he was seriously
injured. Arriving at Norton, witness related the
circumstances to Mr Chapman, Station Master, and
Parsons, the guard. By their advice Stone was taken to
Taunton where he was driven in a cab to the Hospital.
Witness's opinion was that Stone's head came into
contact with one of the girders of the bridge.*

*It was the custom on these engines to use the safety
valve for the purpose of cooking and more especially for
warming tea.*

*The Coroner, "That seems to be a dangerous
practice", Witness "All things are dangerous to
venturesome persons". Stone's back must have been*

towards the bridge when he met with the accident. The Coroner, "Stone acted foolishly, at any rate he ought to have seen that no bridge was in sight when he ventured upon the boiler. I have no doubt that the bridge has been passed by Colonel Yolland and the accident appears to be wholly due to Stone's folly". "Was he an old hand?" – Witness, "Yes". The Coroner. "All these accidents happen to old hands, they do not appear to have any thought of danger".

Mr Farrant, Surgeon, said he attended Stone at the Hospital shortly after his admission, and found him suffering from a fractured skull. Direct violence such as coming into contact with a railway bridge would produce such an injury. Stone died the same evening shortly after witness saw him.

A verdict of "Accidental Death" was returned, and a brother of the deceased who was present at the enquiry, said he was perfectly satisfied with the decision.

After the B&ER was taken over by the Great Western, two terrible disasters occurred at Norton Fitzwarren.

About 12.30am on 11th November 1890, signalman George Rice was dealing with the 38-wagon 6.45pm ex-Bristol Down goods which was shunting the sidings. Interestingly, although a standard gauge train, and headed by Standard Goods 0-6-0 No 1100, it was assisted by a broad gauge pilot locomotive. As only one engine was required for shunting, until the train was ready to continue, the broad gauge locomotive was sent a short distance along the Barnstaple line to be out of the way.

Shunting completed, the Down goods crossed to the Up line to allow the 9.55pm ex-Bristol fast Down goods to overtake. When he reached the Up line where his train was to wait, driver Charles Noble changed the headlight from green (then the normal colour of a headlight) to red as a warning to an oncoming train.

When the Down goods had passed, Noble changed the light back to green in anticipation of the signalman giving him the road. However, this did not happen because signalman Rice had completely forgotten about the Down goods on the Up line and accepted a special train conveying passengers and mail from a South African Cape liner, *Norham Castle*, travelling from Plymouth to Paddington. This was the second of two trains, the first only carrying mails, which passed Norton Fitzwarren at midnight.

The second special, consisting of only two eight-wheel coaches and a van hauled by 4-4-0ST No 2051, built by the Avonside Engine Co of Bristol in 1873, was driven by John Scott and fired by John Thomas, both of Exeter. It came hurtling towards Norton Fitzwarren at 60 mph, the driver having no warning of the obstructing goods because its lights were green and not red. Moments before the crash, the goods fireman yelled to his driver, 'Here's a train a-comin' on our line and he's never going to stop!'

Despite the 60 mph impact, the broad gauge locomotive and train remained upright and in line, though the goods train debris made a pile 30 ft high. The

Broad gauge 4-4-0ST No 2051, left, and standard gauge 1100 after a head-on collision at Norton Fitzwarren on 1 November 1890.
J F King Collect

crew of No 2051 were badly, but not fatally, injure Unfortunately 10 of the 50 passengers were killed, an seriously injured. A large proportion of those killed we miners returning to the North of England from Sou African gold mines, many of them having large sums them, one carrying £90 in gold.

Signalman Rice, aged 63, carried the blame for t accident. The poor man had not been well since bei knocked down by a light engine the previous Janua when his ribs and skull were injured. At the time of t accident he had worked in the signalbox for 20 years, h been on duty for five to six hours and had felt 'bad in t head' the whole of that evening.

Some good came of the accident. To prevent repetition, Rule 55 was adopted by all railways in Gre Britain. It ordered that when a train halted at a signal, t driver was to blow his whistle and if the signalman d not lower his board after three minutes in clear weathe or immediately in fog or falling snow, he must send fireman, guard, or shunter to the signalbox to inform t signalman of the train's presence and not leave until collar had been placed over the relevant signal levers prevent a conflicting movement being made. Additional the person sent was to sign the train register.

As the end of the broad gauge was in sight, No 2051 w scrapped, but Standard Goods No 1100 was repaired an returned to service. She was sold to the Government 1916 and sent to Serbia to haul military trains for th Railway Operating Division. She never returned.

The second big disaster at Norton Fitzwarren w remarkable for the fact that it occurred within a few da of the 50th anniversary of the first major accident ther and also for the fact that a second train had a literal hair breadth escape.

No 1100 at Taunton after the accident on 11th November 1890.   *GWR*

No 2051 at Taunton after the accident on 11th November 1890.   *GWR*

On 4th November 1940 No 6028 *King George VI* with 13 vehicles behind the tender drew into the down relief platform at Taunton eight minutes late with the 9.50pm Paddington to Penzance sleeping car express. Shortly after it arrived, the signalman at Taunton Station West signalbox was informed by Athelney Junction that the 12.50am ex-Paddington, a newspaper train of five bogie vans hauled by another 'King' was running ahead of schedule. As it was not booked to call at Taunton, he correctly decided to let it run through on the main line and send the express as far as Norton Fitzwarren on the parallel relief line, instead of crossing the express to the Down main immediately west of the station as was normal practice.

At 3.44 the express drew out of Taunton and shortly after, the newspaper train ran through at about 55 mph. Unfortunately driver Stacey on the express, not realising he was on the relief, mistook the main line signal for his own. Not until the other 'King' drew alongside just before Norton Fitzwarren station did he realise his error. He immediately closed the regulator and applied the brakes, but at 40 mph there was not time to stop before *King George VI* was derailed at the trap points protecting the main line at the spot where the relief line ended.

The first six coaches of the express spread across all four tracks. Of the 900 passengers aboard, 27 were killed, 13 of these being naval ratings, and 75 injured.

Guard Baggett of the newspaper train did not notice the express, but when struck by an object flying through a window, applied his brake and brought his train to a halt just beyond Victory Siding signalbox, a mile beyond Norton Fitzwarren. After a word with the driver, they proceeded carefully to Wellington for a more thorough examination, but found nothing wrong. And the object which hit guard Baggett? A rivet head from the bogie of *King George VI*. The lower panels of the last newspaper van were found to be marked by ballast flung up by the derailed express. The newspaper train had not quite cleared the scene before the derailed coaches crashed across her road, the second coach of the express taking off one of its rear buffers. Had the newspaper train been just a few seconds later, it would have crashed into the crowded coaches with an even more appalling result.

Express engine driver Stacey, uninjured, hurried back three-quarters of a mile to Silk Mill crossing signalbox to protect the line, but his fireman lay dead. The driver was treated sympathetically, for, apart from the difficulties of driving in the blackout, his home at Acton had been damaged by bombing. The Automatic Train Control siren should have warned him as he passed Norton Fitzwarren Relief Down distant at danger, but he must have cancelled it subconsciously.

It is believed locally that the signalman at Taunton Station West box had already set the road for the express to cross from the Down relief to the Down main just west of the station before he received approach advice from Athelney that the newspaper train was near. Unfortunately, so the story goes, he did not wait for the express driver to whistle, thus acknowledging that he had

No 6028 *King George VI*, overturned at Norton Fitzwarren, 5 November 1940. *Author's Collectio*

seen the altered route, before clearing the signals for the express train to travel along the relief line.

A Newfoundland sailor, travelling to Plymouth to joi HMS Drake, the naval shore establishment, at Devonpor wrote this eye-witness account of the accident:

I was asleep at this instant but awoke to find myself hurtling through the air, amid loud crashing sounds, bounding off this, being hit by that, hearing glass splitting under compression and at the same time thinking "My God, we've been bombed!" They say, at a moment like this, all your past life can pass before your mind in a split second. I believe it. Mine did. Just as I felt that I could stand no more and surely must be dead, it all stopped. For a second or two all was quiet. Then I could hear a loud hissing of steam. Quickly there followed the first of the horrifying cries and screams of the injured and dying.

The Paddington to Penzance Express lay completely wrecked and broken within sight of the Norton Fitzwarren signalbox. The first four coaches were completely telescoped and the remainder were nearly all derailed and scattered over both Up and Down main lines. All that remained of the first four coaches was a pile of twisted steel and wood that lay heaped nearly twenty feet high. I had landed on top of this pile, lying face down on a piece of compartment carpet over the splintered woodwork and wreckage. At first I thought I had been blinded because I could see nothing except two whirling coloured designs in front of each eye. They were going in opposite directions. I moved an arm and felt my watch begin to slip off my wrist. I managed to grab it before it fell away and distinctly remember looking at the luminous dial before pushing it into my jumper pocket. It was 4.05am. Gradually I could make out dim outlines around me. It was raining and looking up I could see that there was nothing over my head. I was open to the sky. My first thought was to get out of there as this was a wooden train and a fire might start.

Managing to roll over on my back and then heaving up into a sitting position I felt a sharp pain in my neck. At the same time I saw that my left pant leg was torn open from thigh to ankle. A six inch gash, bone deep, showed on my knee. There was no blood. Shock, I suppose. I fished a handkerchief out of my sleeve and tied up the injured knee. Not knowing that I was in fact seriously hurt I tried to stand up with the intention of helping others. However I could only stand on one leg and with the other could find nothing solid to stand upon. The pain in my neck was increasing rapidly and I had to lay down again and give up the idea of helping anyone. I couldn't even help myself.

By this time the uninjured passengers from the rear of the train had commenced rescue operations and about half an hour later two sailors with a flashlight spotted me and climbed up to my position. With considerable effort they managed to get me down to the roadbed where I was covered with someone's overcoat. There were about 60 stretcher cases lying there awaiting the arrival of ambulances, which had to cross over a muddy field to get to the scene of the wreck. There were about 30 fatal casualties. The chap sitting next to me went straight to the bottom of the wreck. They found him, alive, 24 hours later.

Later in hospital I heard about the one amusing incident of this terrible wreck. It seems that at the crucial moment one sailor was sitting on the john answering the call of nature. As the wreck occurred he was hurled straight through the coach roof and knocked unconscious. When they picked him up his pants were still down around his ankles. He spent six months in hospital recovering from a fractured pelvis and loss of dignity.

No 6028 lay on her left side at Norton Fitzwarren for several days. Rerailed and drawn to Taunton shed on her own wheels, she was lifted and a replacement bogie put on, the original being damaged. Taunton fitters dismantled the motion before she was taken to Swindon.

Following the accident, some trains were diverted and hauled by 2-6-0s reaching Exeter via Dulverton and the Exe Valley line. They travelled engine-first to Dulverton and had to proceed down the Exe Valley branch tender-first, which was strictly against the rules.

Soldiers assisting with rescue work, 5th November 1940.

J F King Collection

Recovery of the wreckage at Norton Fitzwarren after the accident on 5th November 1940.

J F King Collecti

Coaches involved in the collision on 30th April 1907.

Author's Collectio

Driver Stacey was not the first to have a mistaken impression of the line he was on. Only six months before, in the early hours of 9th May 1940, 2-8-0 No 2844 was hauling a Down goods on the goods running loop and its driver believed he was on the relief line. Seeing the relief line signal off, he obeyed it, rather than the goods loop signal which was against him. No 2844 was derailed at the trap point, ploughed down a low embankment and stopped at an alarming angle, several wagons piling up behind and demolishing the relief line signal. Before warning could be given, a Down parcels train headed by No 4936 *Kinlet Hall* scraped past the projecting wreckage of a goods van, damaging windows and paintwork, but did no serious damage.

Early in 1941 a 'King' borrowed from Old Oak Common was run on the relief line from Taunton station to Norton Fitzwarren to check the visibility of signals. Driven by Reg Chudleigh, a senior locomotive inspector accompanied him on the footplate. The inspector was forced to admit that he had very great difficulty in observing signals, particularly where the main line signals were to the right of the relief line. This was not surprising as the signals were, in fact, to the left!

There were the makings of a disaster at the other side of Taunton on 30th April 1907 when the 9.00am passenger train from Chard, consisting of 0-4-2T No 537 and four coaches were struck by an engine emerging from the goods shed whilst shunting. Seven passengers were injured and the goods engine derailed and badly damaged. Three coaches were wrecked.

On 28th October 1949, 57XX class 0-6-0PT No 9718 was shunting at Fairwater yard. Its crew had not checked that the deflector plate over the superheater elements was secure, with the result that when the engine was worked hard, this plate fell over the blast pipe, causing the exhaust steam to come back through the tubes into the firebox and cab. The crew had to bale out quickly, leaving the regulator open. At the end of the headshunt opposite Silk Mill signalbox, No 9718 went through the buffer stops, crossed the road and came to a halt on the rough track leading to the sewage works.

Taunton 0-4-2T No 5812 was involved in a couple of incidents. One day in November 1946, about 5.30am, as steam pressure rose and with the regulator carelessly left open, with no one on the footplate, No 5812 moved slowly along the turntable spur road, hopped over the

Brake van and wagons after going through the buffers at Silk Mill crossing, 28th October 1949. *J F King Collection*

heavy metal stop lugs protecting the end of the line, and pushed a fitter's bench and tools through the shed wall into the main road about 25 feet below. No 5812 came to halt with its buffer beam and smoke box door protruding through the hole, while the pavement below was blocked by bricks and the bench.

In another mishap a few years later, the same engine le[?] Chard Town and proceeded the three miles downhill t[?] Chard Junction, but when driver Dick Thomas applie[?] the brakes, there was no response. No 5812 and th[?] 'B set' went through the buffers, across the road and int[?] the *Chard Road Tavern* car park!

No 4117 (Taunton) de-railed at the shed entrance, March 1947. The locomotive slid down the gradient from the coal stage and de[?] railed on the catch points. The shedmaster, Reg Aston, right, is wearing a trilby hat.

Roger Venning[?]

9. Signalling

The first locking frame in the area was installed at Norton Fitzwarren in 1870. By 1886 there were signalboxes at Bridgwater, Durston, Creech Junction, Taunton (four boxes lettered D, C, B and A, proceeding westwards), Silk Mill, Norton Fitzwarren, Victory Siding and Wellington. Durston, Creech Junction, Taunton C, Silk Mill and Victory Siding boxes could all be switched out, despite the level crossings at the last two locations. The four branches were worked by wooden train staff, or train staff and ticket. Automatic Train Control was installed on the main line in 1931.

	No. of levers	Construction
Cogload	27	Timber
Creech Junction	78	Brick
Taunton East Junction	147	Brick
Taunton West Station	135	Brick
Taunton West Junction	67	Brick
Taunton East Loop	39	Timber
Taunton West Loop	27	Timber
Silk Mill Crossing	53	Brick
Norton Fitzwarren	131	Timber
Victory Siding	23	Brick

Details of signalboxes in the Taunton area

The first box to be replaced under the Taunton modernisation scheme was Creech Junction on 26th July 1931, while the previous weekend, Cogload Junction box had been moved to a temporary position in order that the flyover could be constructed. In October the goods lines were slued further from the station, while on the 18th of that month, a new Down platform was opened at Creech St Michael halt; a month later a new Up platform was brought into use. As the platforms only served the relief (Bristol) lines, local passenger trains proceeding towards Athelney and requiring to stop, had to run on the Bristol track as far as Durston, where they were diverted on to the single track branch, regaining the Langport line at Athelney.

Quadrupling the section from Creech Junction to Taunton East Junction was completed on 13th December 1931; the length to Taunton West Junction was ready on 7th February 1932 and a week later four lines were opened through to Norton Fitzwarren. The only box not replaced by another bearing the same name was Taunton East Station, which closed on 10th April 1932 when its work was superceded by East Junction using motorised points. With the opening of Blinkhorn Sidings a new replacement signalbox was provided at Silk Mill, together with a second set of crossing gates to protect a new shunting spur which ran behind the box.

No 5533 (Taunton) waits by Taunton West Junction signalbox on 7th July 1946. Taunton School is in the background.

Roger Venning

An impressive array of GWR signals – view from the cab of a dmu to Minehead leaving platform 3, 1st February 1969.

W H Harbor

130

Signal gantry west of the station – view from the cab of a dmu to Minehead, 1st February 1969.

W H Harbor

LIST OF SIGNAL BOXES.

Distance Box to Box.		NAME OF BOX.	TIMES DURING WHICH BOXES ARE OPEN.					Whether provided with Switch.
			Weekdays.			Sundays.		
			Opened.		Closed at	Opened at	Closed at	
M.	C.		Mondays.	Other Days.				
—	—	Highbridge						
1	63	Huntspill	As requi	red for traffic	purposes.	—	—	Yes.
1	4	Pottery Siding	Open fo	r calling Trai	ns only.	—	—	Yes.
—	78	Dunball	6.30 a m.	6.30 a.m.	10.30 p.m.	—	—	Yes.
2	26	Bridgwater	—	Continu	ously.	—	—	No.
1	60	Meads Crossing	6. 0 a.m.	—	—	—	6. 0 a.m.	Yes.
2	26	Fordgate	Closed.					Yes.
—	—	Castle Cary						
—	—	Alford	As requi	red for attac	hing and det	aching traffic.		Yes.
4	54	Keinton Mandeville	To op traffic	en only as re or as necessa	quired for at ry to prevent	taching or de delays to trai	taching ns.	Yes.
2	13	Charlton Mackrell	8.30 a.m. 10. 0 p.m.	8.30 a.m. 10. 0 p.m.	4.30 p.m. 6. 0 a.m.	— —	— 6. 0 a.m.	Yes.
3	38	Somerton	—	Continu	ously.	—	—	Yes.
2	0½	Long Sutton and Pitney	To ope 11.0 a.m. Pe	n as necessary nzance to Pad	for attachin dington and	g and detachi to prevent del	ng traffic; for ays.	Yes.
—	—	Hendford						
3	43½	Montacute	3.55 p.m.	3.55 p.m.	5.45 p.m.	—	—	Yes.
2	52	Martock	First	First	Last	1.20 p.m.	Last Train.	No.
5	12	Langport West	Train.	Train.	Train.	1.30 p.m.	Last Train.	No.
3	9½	Curry Rivel Junction	—	Continu	ously.	—	—	Yes.
4	6	Athelney	—	Continu	ously.	—	—	No.
2	12	Durston	—	Continu	ously.	—	—	Yes.
1	5	Cogload	6. 0 a.m.	—	—	—	2. 0 p.m.	Yes.
2	25	Creech Junction	—	Continu	ously.	—	—	Yes.
2	7	Taunton (East Junction)	—	Continu	ously.	—	—	No.
—	38	Taunton (West Station)	—	Continu	ously.	—	—	No.
—	30	Taunton (West Junction)	—	Continu	ously.	—	—	Yes.
—	15	Taunton (East Loop)	—	Continu	ously.	—	—	Yes.
—	23	Taunton (West Loop)	4.30 a.m.	—	—	—	4. 0 p.m.	Yes.
—	64	Silk Mill Crossing	—	Continu	ously.	—	—	No.
—	54	Norton Fitzwarren	—	Continu	ously.	—	—	Yes.
—	75	Victory Siding	—	Continu	ously.	—	—	No.
2	63½	Poole Siding	7. 0 a.m.	7. 0 a.m.	3. 0 p.m.	—	—	Yes.
1	31½	Wellington	—	Continu	ously.	—	—	Yes.
3	61	Whiteball Tunnel	—	Continu	ously.	—	—	No.
—	61	Burlescombe	6. 0 a.m.	—	—	—	6. 0 a.m.	Yes.
2	51	Sampford Peverell	— —	— —	— —	— 10. 0 p.m.	6. 0 a.m. —	Yes.
1	58	Tiverton Junction	—	Continu	ously.	—	—	Yes.
2	12½	Cullompton	— — —	— — —	— — —	— 9.15 a.m. 7. 0 p.m.	6. 0 a.m. 12. 0 noon —	Yes.
2	17	Westcott	—	Clo	sed.	—	—	Yes.
2	1½	Hele	—	Continu	ously.	—	—	No.
1	17	Silverton	8. 0 a.m.	8. 0 a.m.	8. 0 p.m.	—	—	Yes.
1	78¾	Rewe	—	Clo	sed.	—	—	Yes.
1	44½	Stoke Canon Crossing	—	Continu	ously.	—	—	No.
—	28½	Stoke Canon Junction	— —	— —	— —	— 10. 0 p.m.	6. 0 a.m. —	Yes.
2	7½	Cowley Bridge Junction	—	Continu	ously.	—	—	Yes.
—	68½	Exeter (Riverside)—O	—	Contin	uously.	—	—	No.
—	29½	Exeter, (Goods Yd.) via Loop	6. 0 a.m.	—	—	—	10. 0 p.m.	Yes.
—	14	Exeter (West), via Loop	—	Contin	uously.	—	—	No.
—	72¾	Exeter (East)	—	Continu	ously.	—	—	Yes.
—	16¾	Exeter (Middle)	—	Continu	ously.	—	—	No.
—	22½	Exeter (West)	—	Continu	ously.	—	—	No.
—	61	St. Thomas	6. 0 a.m.	6. 0 a.m.	10. 0 p.m.	—	—	Yes.
—	34	City Basin Junction	—	Continu	ously.	—	—	Yes.
1	52	Cotfield	—	Clo	sed.	—	—	Yes.
1	72	Exminster	—	Continu	ously.	—	—	Yes.
1	74	Powderham	—	Clo	sed.	—	—	Yes.
1	66	Starcross	— —	— —	— —	— 10. 0 p.m.	6. 0 a.m. —	Yes.
1	71	Dawlish Warren	—	Continu	ously.	—	—	No.
1	52	Dawlish	— —	— —	— —	— 10. 0 p.m.	6. 0 a.m. —	Yes.
1	39	Parsons Tunnel	Closed.	—	—	—	—	Yes.
1	32	Teignmouth	—	Continu	ously.	—	—	Yes.
—	22	Old Quay	8. 0 a.m.	8. 0 a.m.	4. 0 p.m.	—	—	Yes.
1	64	Bishopsteignton	8. 0 a.m.	4.30 a.m.	10. 0 p.m.	—	—	Yes.
2	19½	Newton Abbot (Hackney)	—	Continu	ously.	—	—	Yes.
—	41½	Newton Abbot (East)	—	Continu	ously.	—	—	No.
—	31½	Newton Abbot (West)	—	Continu	ously.	—	—	No.
1	3	Aller Junction	—	Continu	ously.	—	—	No.

O—Yard Box.

Signalbox information from the GWR service timetable appendices, 1945

To help the movement of trains at Taunton, if a signal had not been lowered about a minute before a passenger train was ready to leave, the person in charge of the platform had to call the attention of the signalman by means of a push button. In order that platform staff were aware of what train was approaching, the 'Is Line Clear?' signals received by the East Junction and West Station boxes, had to be passed on to the platforms by a code of warning bells as shown in this extract from the Exeter Division Working Timetable of February 1947.

TAUNTON.
Platform Warning Bells.

The " Is Line Clear ? " signals received by East Junction and West Station Boxes for trains stopping at Taunton must be passed on to the Station by the following code on the warning bells :

	Beats.
Express	1
Local	2
Yeovil	3
Chard	4
Minehead	3
Barnstaple	4
Perishable or Parcels	5

Push Bell Communication between Platforms and Signal Boxes.

Push bell communication is provided as under :—

From Platform.	Where Situated.	To Signal Box.
Down Relief Line	East end of Platform	East Junction.
" " "	Outside Down Cloak Room	West Station.
" " "	Near Water Column	" "
Island	East end of Verandah	East Junction.
" " "	At Lift Tower	West Station.
Up Relief Line	East end of Platform	East Junction.
" " "	Opposite Inspectors' Office fixed in telephone box ..	" "

When a train is ready to leave the Station, if the signal has not already been lowered, the person in charge of the platform at which the train is standing must call the attention of the Signalman by using the push bell. The following code rings must be employed :

To West Station Box.		To East Junction Box	
Down Relief	1	Up Relief	1
Down Relief to Main ..	1-2	Up Relief to Main ..	1-2
Barnstaple Bay	2	Up Bay	2
Minehead Bay	3	Up Main	3
Down Main	4	Chard Bay Line ..	4

Should it be necessary to cancel one of the above signals, the Cancelling Signal 3 pause 5 must be sent.

WAREHOUSING

GWR

STORE ON RAILS—
INCREASE YOUR SALES

BOOK YOUR SPACE
WHILE YOU CAN

GREAT WESTERN WAREHOUSES ARE FILLING UP!

Modern Warehouses, electrically equipped for the handling of merchandise, are available at strategic points throughout Great Western territory; in London (South Lambeth, Paddington, and Brentford waterside), at Birmingham, Birkenhead, Bristol, Cardiff, Paignton, Swansea, Taunton, Swindon, etc.

Rent a space—the charges are very low—and maintain a stock for your adjacent customers. Leave the rest to us; we will execute your orders, performing any services such as sampling, labelling, stocktaking, etc. We can by arrangement undertake sales.

Alternatively, if you prefer it, office accommodation is available for your staff to perform the necessary services. Temporary warehouses provide accommodation in country districts for seasonal traffics.

This scheme can SAVE YOU MONEY and EXTEND YOUR BUSINESS. The Chief Goods Manager, Great Western Railway, Paddington Station, London, W.2 (Paddington 7000, extension 2465), will send his representative to discuss the matter with you.

Paddington Station, W.2.   JAMES MILNE, General Manager.

GWR advertisement in *The Railway Gazette*, 30th August 1935

10. The Goods Depot at Taunton: 1930–1965

Once the upgrading of passenger facilities at Taunton was completed, work was started on improving the goods depot. The relatively small brick goods shed on the Down side of the goods loop was demolished and traffic handled at a temporary timber building. The new brick-built goods shed, almost double the size of the old, opened on 20th February 1932, its two platforms connected by movable balance bridges. In order to avoid these being damaged, wagons were not permitted to be shunted into or out of the shed until the shunter in charge of operations had received an assurance from the shed foreman that the bridges had been lifted clear of the tracks. At the east end of the goods shed was a flat-roofed warehouse, 150 ft by 60 ft.

The two through shed roads were known as No 1 and No 2 roads, the second extending beyond the covered confines of the shed to the loading bank which housed a six-ton capacity fixed manual crane. This bank dealt with container traffic and other heavy consignments which required the use of the crane. Inside the goods shed, the highly versatile Swindon-made standard two-wheel platform hand barrow in the hands of an expert could tackle almost every need. One skilled person could manoeuvre objects of considerable weight and size from almost inaccessible places with the aid of rollers and a

Swindon barrow. Although the whole length of the shed was served by overhead gantry cranes consisting of manual block and tackle with a capacity of one ton, these were no use for unloading from vans such items as five-cwt rolls of lead, or four-cwt boxes of bacon, the van roofs preventing the use of a crane.

The extensive overhead warehouse was equipped with two electrically-powered lifts, each with a load capacity of three tons SWL. This accommodation was used mainly for storing animal feed stuffs and allocated under orders from the various representatives of Messrs Bibby, BOCM, Silcock, Crosfield and Lever Brothers, keeping a warehouse checker and assistant in full-time occupation in the replenishment and allocations for this store. The warehouse was also a repository for consignments of a 'To Call For' nature, ranging from personal effects to wines and spirits for the district's gentry. Each firm using the building was charged on the basis of the space occupied, and at regular intervals during the years, tests were taken known as 'The Measuring of Fixed Space', in order to ascertain that it was paid for. Stock records were kept up-to-date; every firm using the warehouse had its own printed stocksheets and it was the duty of the warehouse checker to maintain the movement in and out of store of the various commodities.

In March 1947, a long Down goods to Newton Abbot passes Forty Steps Bridge on the goods loop, hauled by 2-8-2T No 7243 (Wolverhampton, Oxley). On the left is the Avimo factory where important optical instruments were made for the RAF in WWII.
Roger Venning

The goods depot offices in Canal Road had two storeys – the ground floor holding the accounts office, document and stationery store, and toilets. The upper floor housed the general office, the chief clerk working behind a glass partition, while off the hall was the goods agent's office. Twelve clerks were employed, two lady typists and two messengers, another boy messenger being the weighbridge attendant. The early turn messenger started at 5.30am and assisted the early turn clerical staff preparing delivery sheets and their allocation to the separate cartage checkers. After a meal break from 8.30 to 9.30, he went to the mileage office for the inwards wagon books and from these records made out advice notes for general merchandise, coal and coke. On a GWR bicycle he delivered these advice notes to customers responsible for clearing the wagons, ensuring that a signature acknowledging receipt was obtained. This was essential as, if containing general merchandise, a 'free period' of 48 hours was allowed for clearing a wagon and 72 hours for coal and coke. If a wagon had not been emptied beyond this time, daily demurrage charges were incurred at the rate of nine shillings, and six shillings respectively. Traders disliked demurrage and challenged its imposition, considering that the charge smacked of miserliness, whereas from the railway company's perspective, a wagon still under load deprived the railway of its use and therefore loss of revenue.

All goods conveyed by rail required an invoice and involved a great deal of labour-intensive clerical work. In the latter part of World War Two, a system of 'weight only' invoicing was introduced for general merchandise through wagon-loads continuing to be invoiced until the 1960s. All cash received by the goods department was taken to the booking office by the goods office clerk.

In the mid-1930s Taunton goods depot operated a two-shift system: early turn from 5.30am to 2.30pm, and late turn from 2.00pm to 11.00pm. The early turn was known as the inwards gang and the late turn as the outwards gang. Ideally the inwards gang completed discharging all wagons before their shift finished, but when traffic was unusually heavy, the outwards gang helped to complete the off-loading before starting their outwards loading. Inwards consignments had to be checked against invoices, and outwards consignments against customers' consignment notes. There was a brisk trade in 'returned empties' which consisted of wooden boxes and crates of various shapes and sizes to be re-cycled. So heavy was this traffic that wagons were dispatched on a regular basis to 'returned empties' depots at Paddington (Ladbroke), Bristol (Canon's Marsh) and Birmingham (Small Heath). These consignments enjoyed a special 'returned empties rate' on the basis that when full of goods they had arrived by rail; alas this was not always the case, but it was most difficult to prove to the contrary.

Demurrage on Railway Companies' Trucks and Sheets—*continued.*

DEMURRAGE ON COMPANIES' TRUCKS.—The Traders to be allowed a free period of three clear days exclusive of date of arrival in the case of trucks (excluding trucks containing Coal and Coke traffic) standing on the Companies' premises, and four clear days exclusive of date of arrival in the case of trucks on Traders' private sidings or in the Docks, the Trader thereafter to pay 1s. 6d. per ordinary truck per day. On waggons specially constructed to carry heavy weights the ordinary Clearing House Charges, as per C. H. Regulation 372, to apply, viz. :—

	£	s.	d.	
Over 12 tons and under 15 tons...		3	0	After free periods shown in C.H. Reg. 377.
15 tons and under 20 tons..		6	0	
20 „ „ 30 „		12	0	
30 tons and above		1	0	0

If used for a load which could be conveyed on a waggon of less capacity, the rate allowed is regulated by the weight of the load.

DEMURRAGE ON COMPANIES' SHEETS.—The same free periods to be allowed as in the case of trucks, a charge of 6d. per sheet per day to be thereafter paid by the Trader.

Notes—(i.) Sundays, Christmas Day, Good Friday, and Bank Holidays are not to be included in the computation of time

(ii.) The free periods referred to to be treated as the maximum, and the charges referred to as the minimum in each case.

The foregoing arrangements apply also to Forwarded traffic.

Demurrage on Railway Companies' Trucks and Sheets—*continued.*

On the Stock of Companies other than those named on page 3 the following arrangements will apply :—

On traffic carried at rates which do not include handling, not unloaded within 48 hours after despatch of Advice Note, charges of 3s. per ordinary truck per day, and 1s. per sheet per day, must be paid for demurrage; *for example*, Goods arriving on Monday and not removed before closing time on Wednesday would become subject to the charge.

Charges on other Trucks must be paid as under, viz. :—

On Trucks constructed to carry—	Per day. £ s. d.
15 tons and under 20 tons	0 6 0
20 tons and under 30 tons	0 12 0
30 tons and above	1 0 0

On traffic carried at rates which do not include handling, forwarding orders not having been received within 48 hours after being loaded, charges of 3s. per ordinary truck per day, and 1s. per sheet per day, must be paid for demurrage; *for example*, Goods loaded on Monday in respect to which forwarding orders have not been received before closing time on Wednesday would become subject to the charge.

Charges on other Trucks must be paid as under, viz. :—

On Trucks constructed to carry—	Per day. £ s. d.
15 tons and under 20 tons	0 6 0
20 tons and under 30 tons	0 12 0
30 tons and above	1 0 0

An extract from the GWR's *General Instructions* of 1st February 1908

s Taunton handled an exceptional volume of livestock, tle pen accommodation was increased in the 1930s. new cattle dock was opened at the east end of the goods ot conveniently near the market. With the opening of s new dock, two cleaning sidings were established at rty Steps Bridge, just west of the passenger station. unton was a centre for cleaning cattle wagons, local tions sending them to be cleaned after every trip. ydrants were set at various locations and the first eration was washing out the effluent with a high-wered hose. Next, they were swept with a special type brush having metal bristles and finally the van was infected. To avoid the ballast getting drenched, the nning rails were set in concrete, a centre channel ding to drains. Two men were engaged full-time shing cattle wagons, supplemented as necessary by ree or four men from the supernumerary pool. It was t unusual to see 40 to 50 cattle wagons (telegraph code me 'Mex') waiting to be cleaned.

During this period, inwards traffic at Taunton mainly nsisted of large consignments of coal and coke with ecial sidings provided for unloading and distribution local coal merchants. Until the 1960s almost all the cal industrial firms used coal as their main source of wer, as did householders who relied on this fuel for

domestic heating. In the interests of safety, petroleum products were dealt with at special sidings. General merchandise arriving in wagon-loads included building materials and farm supplies, the latter ranging from items such as fertiliser, basic slag, grain, seeds, slabs of cotton seed cake and other animal feed stuffs to implements. Hides and skins for the local tannery were all unloaded at the goods depot or sidings separated by paved roadways to allow lorries access for unloading. The GWR as a common carrier by law was obliged to convey all goods offered and its rate books were required to be open to the general public on request, including to its competitors, the road transport hauliers.

Container traffic, with local delivery or collection by railway-owned motor lorry, was used for household removals and also for frozen meat which came mainly from Avonmouth and London Docks to the local cold store in Laycroft Road. Each Tuesday and Thursday, representatives of the various wholesale meat companies – Armour, Swift, and Weddel – came to the goods shed and sold meat to the trade from insulated meat vans (code name 'Mica'), each firm having its own. The vans which arrived on a Tuesday were filled with orders made the previous Thursday; those on Thursday contained Tuesday's orders. Biscuit manufacturers – Huntley & Palmer, McVitie & Price, Carr's of Carlisle and Macfarlane Lang – all sent Lift Vans (small containers) to Taunton about thrice weekly. These were emptied on to the goods shed platform, lifting only being carried out at the firms' premises. The goods depot also dealt with the return of empty biscuit tins, refilling being very much in fashion. Macfarlane Lang's products were delivered to shops in a GWR-owned vehicle painted in the biscuit firm's livery; the GWR also supplied the driver and van guard, an early example of contract hire.

Outwards traffic from Taunton was also of a wide variety, though tended to be connected with the land. There was a heavy live cattle traffic throughout the year. when cattle sales were held at Bampton, East Anstey, Bishops Nympton & Molland and South Molton, cattle specials were run, the Mex wagons being returned to yards at Taunton to be marshalled into freight trains for delivery to sundry destinations throughout the country. Fresh meat was collected in insulated containers each Tuesday and Thursday from local abattoirs for transit to Smithfield Market. From October to March a huge amount of sugar beet was sent to the Kidderminster factory of the British Sugar Beet Corporation, and also to Kingswinford near Wolverhampton for jam making. Other outwards traffic included butter and eggs; some potatoes and greenstuffs; and locally-cut pit props which were packed manually into five-plank open wagons.

During the season, a train consisting of two bogie vans, one of which had a brake compartment, ran to South Molton three days a week, usually hauled by a 55XX class 2-6-2T. On its return journey, several stops were made to load crates of dead rabbits for delivery to London or Birmingham. This traffic ceased on the outbreak of myxomatosis which decimated the rabbit population.

Hauled by No 5358 (Bristol, St Philip's Marsh), a Down freight consisting of empty cattle trucks passes the bleak winter countryside near Obridge, east of Taunton, in February 1947.
Roger Venning

Most branch freight trains carried 'station trucks', that is four-wheeled vans usually coupled near the engine and unloaded at the passenger platform of smaller stations, but in the case of larger centres such as Minehead and Barnstaple, a complete van or vans would be detached and placed in the goods shed for unloading, empty vans being collected the next day. The GWR promised 'One Day Transits between Important Towns' and kept its promise. A trader in a West Somerset village could ring his supplier in Bristol before noon on a weekday and the goods he ordered be at his local station next morning.

Wagons were received daily at Taunton from various London depots – Paddington, South Lambeth, Park Royal, Victoria & Albert Docks – while other daily arrivals came from Bristol Temple Meads, Bristol Lawrence Hill, Birmingham, Manchester, Cardiff and depots in the West of England. Branch lines to Yeovil and Chard were also served by the station truck system. Each station truck was loaded in accordance with a printed diagram displayed on the side of the van. Staff at various stations and depots knew where to look for their own consignments and where to place goods for other stations along the line.

Many years ago, habitual pilfering was experienced from consignments of tobacco carried on one of the branch line trucks. The Railway Police were alerted and the local detective based at Taunton decided to conceal himself in a large laundry basket which had been specially provided. He kept observations on all the operations at the various stations along the branch and eventually discovered the culprit, but *en route* was given a few rough shunts by the train crew who knew of his mission.

All traffic sent as 'Smalls' and 'Through Truck-Loads' was subject to individual invoicing and, until 1941, goods could be dispatched on 'Carriage Forward To Pay'. Where consignments in through truck-loads were sent to be weighed at Taunton, a PTF (Particulars To Follow) invoice was issued to the receiving point by the sending station and, when the weighing slip had been received, a fully charged invoice would be issued to clear the PTF. The truck weighbridge at Taunton was near the Chard bay, platform 2, at the east end of the Down passenger platform. Wagons were sent from branch line and some main line stations labelled 'To Weigh', an operation carried out by the yard shunting staff. A lad messenger visited the weighbridge and sent off weighing slips to the stations concerned who used them for charging purposes.

Until 1st June 1947, 'Smalls' traffic was carried in station trucks, but on this date, most station truck working was abolished and replaced by zonal C&D (collection and delivery). A pilot scheme had been carried out in Cornwall and as it proved successful, was extended eastwards. Although some through wagons still ran to Taunton's sub-railheads at Bridgwater, Minehead and Langport West, any goods unloaded at Taunton were not sent on by rail, but dispatched to these three depots by trunk road motor. Minehead and Langport West still received through wagons from Bristol and Paddington,

but from other centres 'Smalls' were sent to Taunton a carried onwards by trunk road motor. Wellington C& was from Taunton, two Thornycroft 'Nippy' eight-t articulated vehicles being used. To Wellington the lo seldom exceeded four tons, but returning with goo from factories it was six to eight tons.

The main function of the zonal C&D system was eliminate small consignments of freight traffic fro wayside and branch line stations, keeping them only f full truck loads. Small consignments were concentrat at railheads or sub-railheads.

From June 1947, outwards traffic which had be previously loaded out from the goods shed, was de with in the mileage yard on Nos 5 & 6 roads. Abo 30–35 vans stood on these lines marked to vario destinations. Motor drivers with consignments to forwarded would call at the outwards office, formerly t mileage office, have the consignments coded to t requisite numbered van and then, accompanied by checker, load the consignments accordingly. Th system, known as 'Outwards Perambulation', continu in operation until 1963 when Taunton became a Freigh Concentration Depot.

The perambulation system had its faults and was n popular for a number of reasons. Staff were obliged work in the open in all winds and weather, and in rai weather the interior of the railway vans became very we to avoid this, much opening and closing of doors wa necessary which made extra work. Damage by rain an other causes led to a sharp increase in claims by customer Also, with the loading of heavy and awkward objects it wa necessary for road vehicles to 'tail' in to the railway van but this was not always possible under congeste conditions. As a result it was a risky business handlin heavy consignments under these circumstances an various accidents occurred resulting in personal injury.

The zonal C&D system continued until 1963 whe Taunton became a Freight Concentration Depot, th sub-railhead depots being closed. The development motorways and supermarkets with their own roa transport, led to the end of freight at Taunton, lack traffic causing the depot to close in 1972.

The early 1930s saw the introduction of the countr lorry service which developed into a useful contributio to the lives of those living in rural areas. Until i introduction, delivery by railway vehicles was restricte to within the town area. A country lorry service catere for passenger train parcels as well, so after loading at th goods depot, lorries also called at the parcels office During the 1930s, mail order firms developed their trad and sent goods by rail, greatly increasing the workloa of the country lorry service. Consignments labelled 'T Call For' were kept at the depot, but others wer delivered and charges collected. On consignment invoiced 'Paid Home', delivery was recharged to th sending station on the 'Station Ledger Transfer'.

The former stables, used until 1932 by the GWR local carting agent F W Barber, became a small garage officially known as the Road Motor Engineers

While waiting for clear signals on the goods loop at the East yard in mid-February 1947, WD No 77161 (Plymouth, Laira) takes water and is oiled. Notice the Westinghouse brake pump beside the smokebox and the 'home-made' smoke deflector on the chimney.

Roger Venning

Ex-Railway Operating Division No 3019 (Westbury) with an Up fast freight train taking water at the East yard in April 1947.

Roger Venning

A main line stopping goods train, having used the goods loop, is held by signals at the East Loop signalbox on 11th September 1947. 'Dukedog' No 9019 (Birmingham, Tyseley) has a 2,000 gallon tender, whereas most of the class had one with a capacity of 3,000 or 3,500 gallons.

Roger Venning

Horse van lettered 'GWR' belonging to carting agent F W Barber, in North Street, c.1906. The Taunton & West Somerset Electric Railways & Tramways Company Limited's line opened on 21st August 1901 from the east end of East Reach to the GWR station. It was extended to Rowbarton on 13th August 1909.
Author's Collection

Department. Manned by a foreman fitter and two assistants, they maintained all vehicles within a 15-mile radius, major overhauls being undertaken by the RME at Exeter. The fleet, mostly manufactured by Thornycroft, consisted of many vehicles over 15 years old, some even having seen military service in World War One and, until 1936, ran on solid tyres. The older vehicles had open fronts, the only shelter from the elements being a tarpaulin to cover the lower part of the driver in bad weather, the van guard's seat being merely a small wooden plank. Pallets had yet to arrive, and the only effort at modernisation was the introduction of three and four-wheeled tractor units allowing trailers to be left for unloading or loading, while the tractor hauled a trailer elsewhere. Although larger vehicles could carry up to eight tons, most could only take a load of three or four. The majority of these smaller vehicles were open at the side. Windscreen wipers were hand-operated and an instruction in the cab read: 'Open the windscreen if you cannot obtain a clear view'.

Although many of the vehicles used were basic, a few were well-equipped. Around 1935 a new AEC Monarch arrived. Fleet No 3409, registration BLB 509, it had leather-upholstered, adjustable seats. Other vehicles included a 1920 vintage six-ton ADC (Associated Daimler Company) lorry and Morris Commercial two-ton van No 2826, registration ALN 370, which on Mondays, Wednesdays and Fridays delivered in the Quantock area, and Tuesdays, Thursdays and Saturdays

in the Blackdown Hills. Tractor units were of the three and six-ton Scammell and three-ton Karrier Cob variety.

Some of the traffic, such as sugar beet, required specialised vehicles. Railway staff using a GWR Fordson tractor and trailer called at a farm and tossed the beet into the trailer. The GWR general stores in Swindon supplied special sugar beet forks in late September; these had nine tines with bulbous ends to prevent the beet being damaged. One of these forks was heavy enough on its own but when loaded with beet and swung with sufficient impetus to throw the contents over the trailer sides, it was very tiring work indeed. When travelling, the tractor driver and his mate had no protection whatsoever from the weather and on a wet day became soaked. In the 1930s the tractor driver was paid £2.17.6 and his mate £2.10.0. On arrival at the siding the pair had to tranship the beet by hand into railway wagons. If there was a sufficient number of loaded trucks, a complete train was dispatched, otherwise they were sent by ordinary freight train. Growers sending beet to the BSC factory were controlled by a permit scheme which determined when their beet should be offered to rail for transit; this method ensured that the railway and factory did not become overburdened.

When a cattle 'Collection & Delivery Service' for conveying livestock to and from markets and farms was instituted at Taunton in the 1930s, two road vehicles were used and dealt with work involving both Taunton, which had its market day on Saturday, and Exeter, where

GWR advertisement from the 1930s

the market was held on Friday. Between market days work was 'on offer' – such as collecting pigs from outlying farms and taking them to the bacon factory in Taunton. These two vehicles, a Morris Commercial two-ton short-wheelbase truck hauling a trailer, and a three-ton Thornycroft 'Nippy', were also used for moving livestock to and from agricultural shows.

Pit props cut from Forestry Commission land on the Blackdown Hills were carried on a three-ton AEC and trailer. Although restricted to 12 mph, the driver was not averse to placing the vehicle in neutral and free-wheeling downhill, twice in one week being caught by the police for speeding, the prosecution claiming that he had achieved 27 mph. For a short period, timber was collected from the same plantation by a Latil tractor and pole carriage. Unlike the GWR's Fordson tractors, the driver and mate travelled in a completely closed cab. The Latil was highly efficient with four-wheel drive and quad steering. The road motor staff were sorry when it was soon transferred away from Taunton. The private contractor carrying out the felling and sawing helped to load the railway lorries. According to the contract,

collection should have been from a 'hard road site', but this was not always possible and it was not unknown for the GWR vehicle to become bogged down, wasting many hours throughout the contract.

During the thirties and early forties, delivery of much of the local goods around the town was by horse and dray with a carman in charge, six horses being stabled at Taunton until the early 1950s. Horse carmen and motor drivers had it stressed on them that they were the railway company's ambassadors and must show every respect to customers' wishes.

Typical loads were cigarettes in wood or cardboard boxes, casks of china, rolls of lead and barrels of vinegar. All supplies for Boots the Chemist arrived by rail in wooden crates, some very heavy. Weighty goods were offloaded using cartage skids – two lengths of wood about seven feet long, with a hook at one end to catch on the side of the dray, the other resting on the ground. Goods were then slid down the two strips of wood, with chain keeping the lengths from spreading too wide apart.

Immediately before and in the early months of World War Two, vast amounts of building materials were delivered to Taunton to set up military camps, three airfields including hangars and food buffer depots, in addition to the military stores at Blinkhorn. To lift the iron and steel girders, the railway obtained a Ransome & Rapier mobile crane. Until its arrival, all lifting was carried out by a fixed manual crane. These buildings demanded thousands of tons of cement which arrived in hessian or paper sacks, all unloaded by hand; all accommodation sidings within many miles of Taunton were full of wagons awaiting siding space at the mileage yard where they could be unloaded. Once constructed the buffer depots were filled with flour, corned beef, dates and other dried fruit which arrived by rail from various ports. Often the vehicles clearing wagons of, say, corned beef, returned with perhaps flour to fill those same wagons. It was tiring work shifting these goods and at a time of food rationing, the only extra sustenance those men received was a small increase in their weekly cheese allowance. Goods were generally moved on two-wheel sack trucks, each taking either one sack, or four cases.

By 8.00am each morning a queue of 'casual' workers or 'supers' (supernumeraries), as they were called, formed outside the goods depot offices and many were employed for the day to assist with extra heavy traffic. Availability of work for these supers depended on the supervisory foreman's summing up of the work load for that day. Increased demand for cattle wagons could mean that additional assistance was required on the cattle wagon washing platform and men would be taken on to cover that work. Wagons given a red card because of a defect had to be taken out of service and their loads transhipped – again, this was a task for casual labour. On a busy day, ten men might be taken on. Then in 1939 when many of the permanent staff were called-up on mobilisation of the Territorial Army, there was a serious lack of skilled manpower and many of the 'regular casuals' were appointed to the permanent staff.

Inside the Inspector's Office at Taunton East goods yard, .1950: Area Inspector Bert Loveys, Yard Inspector C James and shunter C Weasley. *Tony Harvey*

Throughout the war years the goods depot staff were under a great strain ensuring that wagons were speedily discharged and the goods they contained delivered with the minimum of delay, especially military equipment and food. This was not their only responsibility for in 1940, soon after the evacuation from Dunkirk, the GWR set up its own company of Local Defence Volunteers, later to become the Home Guard; local railwaymen guarded stations, yards, bridges and tunnels against the expected attack from German paratroopers. Almost unarmed at

Some Taunton staff in 1948 pose in front of 0-6-0PT No 1909 (Taunton): left to right – shunter Jack Kearl, guard Tony Harvey and shunter Maurice Bradford. *Tony Harvey Collection*

first, they were later supplied with a Webley .45 revolver and two rounds of ammunition.

Taunton goods clerical staff in 1896. *J F King Collection*

No 9718 (Taunton) with a branded shunters' truck (known as 'chariots' at Taunton), in the West yard, 24th February 1945. The box on top contains flags, re-railing ramps and tools. A steel plate between running board and wheel prevents shunters' feet, or poles, being damaged by the wheel spokes.

Peter Short

Taunton Ambulance Class of 1890.

J F King Collection

One night when guarding the approach to Taunton station, one of the porters on duty told members of the railway Home Guard that a special train had arrived at an Up platform loaded with French sailors under armed guard. They were crews of French warships which had mutinied at Devonport Dockyard when the Royal Navy fired on the French fleet at Oran. The train was in a state of chaos with many broken windows and blood stains. Another task for the Taunton railway Home Guard Company was to man an anti-aircraft gun to defend the station against air attack.

The East yards were situated on the Up and Down sides of the goods loop and had their own signalbox. Incoming goods trains to the Down side yard came from such diverse origins as Paddington Goods, South Lambeth, Park Royal, Victoria & Albert Docks, Acton – where traffic was collected from the other three Regions – Banbury, Oxley Sidings, Scours Lane Reading, Avonmouth and South Wales. From the Midlands, traffic was transferred by the London Midland Region to Bristol West depot. Trains from these various starting points generally detached wagons for Taunton and/or the local branch lines, together with wagons for stations between Taunton and Highbridge, and Taunton and Tiverton Junction, which were taken to their destination by a local freight. Goods trains for the Barnstaple branch

were made up at the Down side yard, while wagons for the Minehead branch and intermediate stations to Dulverton or South Molton were transferred to the West yard for marshalling into separate trains. Wagons for intermediate stations between Taunton and Tiverton Junction were taken to Fairwater yard, as was any traffic which could not be accommodated in the Down side yard. Wagons placed in the Down side yard for the Chard and Yeovil branches and intermediate stations to Highbridge were transferred to the Up side yard.

In the forties and fifties the numbers of local or branch freights leaving Taunton daily were as in the table below.

No. of Trains	Destination
4	Barnstaple
1	South Molton
1	Dulverton
1	Highbridge
2	Minehead
1	Yeovil
2	Chard
1	Tiverton Junction

In addition to the loaded wagons marshalled into these trains, empty or specialist wagons would also be conveyed, provided that maximum loads were not exceeded. These wagons were ordered by various outstations and given to the goods yard foreman who ensured that the head shunter fulfilled the requirements.

Marshalling a freight train demanded skill and was not just a matter of seeing that wagons were in station order; their position in the train depended on which end of th station the sidings were situated. For example, althoug Bishops Lydeard was one of the first stops for th Minehead goods, traffic for this station was marshalled the rear as due to the sidings facing Down trains, it wa easiest to uncouple the engine, run round the train an detach the guard's van and wagons, shunt the latter, re attach the brake van and then run the engine to the fro

WD No 79226 (Birkenhead) with a Down freight on the goods loop, on 20th September 1947. Notice the WD and arrow on the tender. In the background is the coaling stage.

Roger Venning

SOUTHERN RAILWAY.

(9/34)   TO   Stock 787

TAUNTON

Via _____

11. Named Trains

The most famous named train to pass through Taunton was the 'Cornish Riviera Express'. It started with the introduction of the first regular non-stop Paddington to Plymouth service on 1st July 1904. It soon began to service intermediate stations by means of slip coaches dropped at Westbury for Weymouth, Taunton for Minehead and Ilfracombe, and Exeter for Torquay, Brent and Kingsbridge. This system had the advantage of allowing a shorter and lighter train over the steep gradients west of Taunton and between Newton Abbot and Plymouth, while greater loads could be hauled over the flatter terrain east of those points. The 'Cornish Riviera' provided a quick service to Taunton; in 1910, the slip coach arrived at 1.00pm, 2½ hours after leaving Paddington.

Before 1939 the 'Cornish Riviera' slipped five coaches at Taunton: the first two for Ilfracombe, and the last three for Minehead. The rear three were picked up by the East End shunter and placed behind the 1.05pm to Minehead, the other two being left on the Down main.

The 1.10pm to Barnstaple moved out from the bay platform and reversed on to the slip coaches, leaving from this Down main platform. The slip coaches were then of the single-ended variety.

On at least one occasion the guard forgot to slip. The driver saw the coaches still on and braked. However the guard released the coaches and the startled driver saw the detached coaches catching up his train, so opened the regulator very quickly, throwing fire out of the chimney. The slip coaches eventually stopped by the West sidings and were collected by the shunter.

The 'Cornish Riviera' was usually composed of the company's very best rolling stock. Soon after the express's inauguration, it was made up of 70-ft long elliptical-roofed stock of 'clipper' outline with recessed end doors only. This was replaced successively by flush-sided 70-ft vehicles with side doors; then by 60-ft coaches; and in 1935 with 'Centenary' stock, again of maximum width with recessed end doors. In 1951 the new BR Standard Mark 1 rolling stock appeared.

The Up 'Cornish Riviera Express', in the new BR standard livery, passes Norton Fitzwarren on 6th April 1950. The unrecorded 'King' is in blue livery and the coaches in red and cream.   *Pursey Short*

No 6018 *King Henry VI* (Newton Abbot) with the Down 'Cornish Riviera Express' passing Fairwater Bridge, August 1947.

Another well-known train was the 'Torbay Express'. At first this left Paddington at 11.50am and, like the 'Cornish Riviera', slipped coaches at Taunton for Ilfracombe. It was the only slip portion ever to have included a Restaurant Car in its four-coach formation. Soon after the outbreak of World War Two, the Down 'Torbay Express' and the 'Cornish Riviera' were amalgamated, but the combined load proved too great and separate trains left ten minutes apart. In the summer of 1946 its old departure time of 12.00 noon from Paddington was restored, the train running non-stop to Exeter.

Both these expresses date from the early years of the 20th century, but back in the 1840s the 9.50am Paddington to Exeter was retimed and named after the racehorse which in 1849 won both the Derby and the St Leger. The 'Flying Dutchman', carrying only first and second class passengers, now left Paddington at 9.30am and arrived at Bristol three hours later, running from Bristol to Taunton non-stop. In October 1867 the GWR experienced financial problems and one economy was the 'Flying Dutchman' which was suspended for 18 months. In 1871 it was speeded up to cover the 44.8 miles Bristol to Taunton in 51 minutes – an average speed of 52.7 mph. At last in 1890, third class passengers were allowed to travel on this train, which ceased running in 1911.

In 1955 two rather inauspicious named trains appeared – the 'Mayflower' and 'The Royal Duchy'. The headboard of the former carried a picture of the ship of that name, while the latter displayed the relevant coat of arms. Ten years later, more intensive use of rolling stock and the associated shorter times spent at the termini, meant that fixing or detaching nameboards was a nuisance and so these trains were abolished.

As well as some of the Paddington to West of England trains being named, so were those from the North. 'The Devonian', begun in 1928, ran from Bradford to Paignton, though for the winter half of the year most of the train terminated at Bristol, with only three coaches running through to Devon, while in the Up direction they were attached to a West of England to the North train between Newton Abbot and Bristol.

To try to ease pressure on the popular 'Cornish Riviera', in the summer of 1935 'The Cornishman' was introduced as a summer-only, exclusively reserved-seat train. However, the idea did not prove to be economic and the train did not appear in the timetables the following summer. In 1952 the name was resurrected and used for the Wolverhampton, Birmingham, Stratford-upon-Avon and Cheltenham to Penzance train, serving Taunton with a slip coach.

The Down 'Torbay Express' passes Norton Fitzwarren hauled by 'Castle' class No 5078 *Beaufort* (Newton Abbot) on 6th April 1950. In the left background is the large United States Army Stores Depot served by Blinkhorn Sidings.   *Pursey Short*

① Cornish Riviera Express

WEEKDAYS AND SUNDAYS

SUNDAYS

	a.m.	a.m.	a.m.
London (Paddington)	10A30	10A30	10A30
	p.m.	p.m.	p.m.
Exeter (St. David's) arr.			2 3
Newton Abbot			2 31
Plymouth (North Rd.)	2 30	3 25	3 35
Liskeard			
Par	3 33		4 45
St. Austell			4 57
Truro	4 3	5 0	5 20
Redruth		5 22	5 44
Camborne		5 32	5 53
Gwinear Road	4 33		
Hayle		5 42	6 3
St. Erth	4 43	5 50	6 10
Penzance	4 55	6 5	6 25

(vertical notes: Runs 22nd Sept. 1957, 18th, 25th May; 1st and 8th June 1958 only — Runs 29th Sept. 1957 to 11th May 1958)

SUNS.

	a.m.	a.m.
Penzance dep.	10A 0	9A45
St. Erth	10A12	9A55
Gwinear Road	10A24	—
Camborne	—	10A11
Truro	10B53	10C38
Par	11B25	11C10
	p.m.	p.m.
Plymouth (North Rd.)	12A30	12A20
Exeter (St. David's)	—	1 50
London (Paddington) arr.	4 40	5 30

A—Seats can be reserved in advance on payment of a fee of 2s. 0d. per seat.
B—From 14th Oct. 1957 to 10th May 1958 Note "A" applies.
C—From 29th Sept. 1957 to 11th May 1958 Note "A" applies.

RESTAURANT CAR SERVICE

---

② Torbay Express

WEEKDAYS

	noon			
London (Paddington) dep.	12A 0	Kingswear dep.	11A25
	p.m.	Churston (for Brixham)	11A35
Exeter (St. David's) arr.	2 52	Paignton	11A48
Torquay	3 35		noon
Paignton	3 48	Torquay	12A 0
Churston (for Brixham)	4 0		p.m.
Kingswear	4 10	Exeter (St. David's)	12 40
		London (Paddington) arr.	3 35

A—Seats can be reserved in advance on payment of a fee of 2s. 0d. per seat.

RESTAURANT CAR SERVICE

---

⑦ The Cornishman

WEEKDAYS (Mondays to Fridays)

	a.m.
WOLVERHAMPTON (Low Level) dep.	9A 0
Bilston Central	9A 6
Wednesbury Central	9A12
West Bromwich	9A20
Birmingham (Snow Hill)	9A40
Stratford-upon-Avon	10 19
Cheltenham Spa (Malvern Road)	11 2
Gloucester Eastgate	11 20
	p.m.
Bristol (Temple Meads) arr.	12 15
Taunton	1 15
Exeter (St. David's)	1 58
Dawlish	2 33
Teignmouth	2 41
Newton Abbot	2 51
Torre arr.	3 8
Torquay	3 11
Paignton	3 21
Goodrington Sands Halt	3B24
Churston (for Brixham)	3 30
Kingswear	3 41
Plymouth (North Road) arr.	3 20
Liskeard	3 59
Bodmin Road	4 15
Par	4 28
St. Austell	4 39
Truro	5 3
Redruth	5 29
Carn Brea	5 34
Camborne	5 40
Hayle	5 50
St. Erth	5 57
Penzance	6 7

	a.m.	a.m.
PENZANCE dep.	10A10	10A30
St. Erth	10A22	10A40
Gwinear Road	10A35	—
Camborne	10A43	—
Redruth	10A52	—
Truro	11A12	11A48
St. Austell	11 37	11 48
Par	11 46	11 57
	p.m.	p.m.
Bodmin Road	12 1	
Liskeard	12 20	
Plymouth (North Road) dep.	1 0	1 0
Kingswear dep.	12A15	12A15
Churston (for Brixham)	12A30	12A30
Goodrington Sands Halt	12B40	12C40
Paignton	12A55	12A55
Torquay	1A 2	1A 2
Torre	1 7	1 7
Kingskerwell	1 15	1 15
Newton Abbot dep.	1 23	1 23
Teignmouth	1 34	1 34
Dawlish	1 42	1 42
Exeter (St. David's)	2 24	2 24
Taunton	3 5	3 5
Bristol (Temple Meads)	4 8	4 8
Gloucester Eastgate arr.	5 3	5 3
Cheltenham Spa (Malvern Road)	5 21	5 21
Stratford-upon-Avon	6 3	6 3
Birmingham (Snow Hill)	6 49	6 49
West Bromwich	7 4	7 4
Wednesbury Central	7 12	7 12
Bilston Central	7 18	7 18
Wolverhampton (Low Level)	7 25	7 25

(vertical notes: Runs 14th October 1957 to 10th May 1958 inclusive — Runs until 12th October 1957 inclusive, and commencing 12th May 1958)

A—Seats can be reserved in advance on payment of a fee of 2s. 0d. per seat.
B—Commences 5th May, 1958.
C—Commences 12th May, 1958.

RESTAURANT CAR SERVICE

---

⑬ The Royal Duchy

WEEKDAYS

	p.m.	p.m.
London (Paddington) dep.	1 A30	1 A30
Reading General	2U13	2U13
Westbury arr.	3 18	3 18
Taunton	4 13	4 13
Exeter (St. David's)	4 53	4 53
	p.m.	p.m.
Newton Abbot	5 27	5 27
Kingskerswell	5 42	5 42
Torre	5 50	5 50
Torquay	5 53	5 53
Paignton	6 6	6 6
Goodrington Sands Halt	6 C10	6 B10
Churston (for Brixham)	6 17	6 17
Kingswear	6 27	6 27
Plymouth (North Road)	6 25	6 25
Liskeard	7 5	7 5
Bodmin Road	7 21	7 21
Lostwithiel	7 28	7 28
Par	7 38	7 38
St. Austell	7 49	7 40
Truro	8 12	8 12
Chacewater		8 27
Redruth	8 33	8 38
Camborne	8 42	8 46
Gwinear Road		8 53
Hayle		9 1
St. Erth	8 57	9 1
Penzance	9 10	9 20

(vertical notes: Runs 14th October 1957 to 10th May 1958 inclusive — Runs until 12th October 1957 inclusive, and commencing 12th May 1958)

	a.m.
Penzance dep.	11A 0
Marazion	—
St. Erth	11A13
Camborne	11A39
Redruth	11A47
Chacewater	—
	p.m.
Truro	12A 1
St. Austell	12 27
Par	12 36
Lostwithiel	12 48
Bodmin	12 57
Liskeard	1 18
Plymouth (North Rd.)	2 0
Kingswear	1A50
Churston (for Brixham)	2A 0
Paignton	2A 9
Torquay	2A18
Torre	2 22
Newton Abbot	2 55
Teignmouth	2 46
Dawlish	2 55
Exeter (St. David's)	3 30
Taunton	4 14
Westbury	5 14
Newbury arr.	6 2
Reading General	6 25
London (Paddington)	7 15

A—Seats can be reserved in advance on payment of a fee of 2s. 0d. per seat.
B—Commences 5th May, 1958.
C—Commences 12th May, 1958.
U—Calls to pick up passengers only.

RESTAURANT CAR SERVICE

---

⑭ The Mayflower

WEEKDAYS

	a.m.			p.m.
Plymouth (North Road) dep.	8 30	London (Paddington) dep.	5A30
Kingswear	8 35	Taunton arr.	7 57
Churston (for Brixham)	8A45	Exeter (St. David's)	8 37
Paignton	8A55	Dawlish	9 15
Torquay	9A 2	Teignmouth	9 25
Torre	9 6	Newton Abbot	9 39
Newton Abbot	9 26	Torre	9 42
Exeter (St. David's)	10 0	Torquay	9 55
Taunton	10 40	Paignton	10 5
Westbury	11 40	Churston (for Brixham)	10 15
	p.m.	Kingswear	10 15
Reading (General) arr.	12C45	Plymouth (North Road)	10 0
London (Paddington)	1 25		

A—Seats can be reserved in advance on payment of a fee of 2s. 0d. per seat.
C—Slip Carriage (Restaurant Car not available).

RESTAURANT CAR SERVICE

Extracts from the Named Trains handbill covering 16th September 1957 to 8th June 1958

BR Standard Class 9F 2-10-0 No 92206 heads the Up 'Mayflower' east of Creech on Saturday 8th August 1959. *John Cornelius*

No 6002 *King William IV* near Creech with the Down 'Royal Duchy', 8th August 1959. *John Cornelius*

No 6019 *King Henry V* leaves Taunton with the 8.30am Plymouth to Paddington express in September 1947. This train was the predecessor of 'The Mayflower'.
Roger Venning

No 7018 *Dryslwyn Castle* at Taunton with the Down 'Cornishman', 11th June 1960.

John Cornelius

John Cornelius

No 7036 *Taunton Castle* entering Taunton station on the Down main, 20th August 1960.

No 2913 *Saint Andrew* stands in the Parish of St Andrew at the Up relief platform with a train for Bristol in 1947.

S P Bowditch Collection

Appendix – Locomotive Allocations

Taunton – May 1922

2-4-0T 'Metro'
456 461 975

0-6-0 'Standard Goods'
504 704

0-4-2T '517' class
545 834 838

0-6-0ST/PT '1076' class
959 966 1181 1575

0-6-0ST/PT '1854' class
1761 1794 1876 1893

0-6-0PT '1813' class
1845

0-6-0ST/PT '850' class
1927 1954

0-6-0 'Dean Goods'
2320 2381 2405 2435 2460 2467 2543

4-4-0 'Bulldog' class
3307 *Exmoor* 3318 *Vulcan* 3363 *Alfred Baldwin*

4-4-0 '3521' class
3532 3547

4-4-0 'Badminton' class
4105 *Earl Cawdor*

4-4-0 'Atbara' class
4124 *Kitchener*

2-6-2T '45XX' class
4505 4525

2-6-0 '43XX' class
5348 6300

Steam Rail Motors
71 77 97 98 99

Total 37 locomotives and 5 rail motors

Bridgwater – May 1922

0-60ST ex-Cornwall Mineral Railway
1397

0-4-2T '517' class
1471

Total 2 locomotives

Taunton – 31st December 1947

0-4-0ST ex-Cardiff Railway
1338 (sub-shedded at Bridgwater)

0-6-0PT '1854' class
1760

0-6-0PT '850' class
1909

4-6-0 'Star' class
4026 4056 *Princess Margaret*

2-6-2T '5101' class
4113 4117 4136 5172

4-6-0 'Hall' class
4954 *Plaish Hall* 5982 *Harrington Hall*
5999 *Wollaton Hall*

'Star' class No 4026 (Taunton), originally named *The Japanese Monarch*, in the coaling queue, June 1947. The ramp on the right was used by locomotive coal wagons supplying fuel to the stage.
Roger Venning

No 5982 *Harrington Hall* (Taunton) arrives at platform 1 with a Bristol to Taunton stopping train on 16th June 1945. Notice the crane in the permanent way yard to the left of the locomotive's smokebox.
Pursey Short

0-6-0PT '2021' class
2038 (sub-shedded at Bridgwater) 2127

0-6-0ST ex BP&GVR
2194 *Kidwelly*

0-6-0 '2251' class
2211 2212 2213 (sub-shedded at Minehead) 2214 2215
2261 2266 (sub-shedded at Barnstaple) 2267 2268
2275 (sub-shedded at Barnstaple)

0-6-0PT '655' class
2708

0-6-0PT '2721' class
2748 2755

2-8-0 '28XX' class
2814

4-4-0 'Bulldog' class
3443 *Chaffinch* 3444 *Cormorant*

2-4-0T 'Metro'
3582

4-6-0 'Castle' class
5003 *Lulworth Castle* 5077 *Fairey Battle*

2-6-2T '4575' class
5501 5503 5504 5521 5522 5533 5542 5543 5571

0-4-2T 'Collett 0-4-2T'
5812

2-6-0 '43X' class
6305 6317 6323 6328 6343 6364 6372 6377 6394
6398 7304 7314

0-6-0PT '74XX' class
7421

0-6-0PT '57XX' class
9718 9757

2-8-0 ex-War Department
WD 77077

4-wheel petrol-engine Service Locomotives
23 24

Total 62 locomotives

Taunton – March 1959

0-4-0ST ex-Cardiff Railway
1338

0-6-0ST '1361' class
1362

0-6-0PT '1366' class
1366

0-6-0PT '16XX' class
1668

0-6-0 '2251' class
2235

2-8-0 '28XX' class
2822

0-6-0PT '8750' class
3669 3736 4604 4663 9608 9646 9647 9663 9670
9671 9718 9757

2-6-2T '5101' class
4128 4157 4159 5185

4-6-0 'Hall' class
4930 *Hagley Hall* 4932 *Hatherton Hall*
4940 *Ludford Hall* 4970 *Sketty Hall*
4971 *Stanway Hall* 4978 *Westwood Hall*
4985 *Allesley Hall* 4991 *Cobham Hall*
5992 *Horton Hall* 5999 *Wollaton Hall* 6995 *Benthall
Hall*

2-6-2T '4575' class
5503 5504 5521 5525 5543 5571

0-6-0PT '57XX' class
5721 5779 5780 5798

2-6-0 '43XX' class
6323 6337 6343 6364 6372 6375 6390 6398 7304

4-6-0 'Grange' class
6815 *Frilford Grange* 6868 *Penrhos Grange*
6874 *Haughton Grange*

0-6-0PT '74XX' class
7436

Total 56 locomotives

No 2194 *Kidwelly* (Taunton), one of the very few named GWR tank engines, shunting by Fairwater Bridge in September 1946.

Roger Venning

Open-back No 2748 (Taunton) shunting at East yard in June 1947.

Roger Venning

Bibliography

Allen, C J, *Titled Trains of the Western* (Ian Allan, 1974)

Alves, J, *Resorts for Railfans: Taunton* (Trains Illustrated, October 1957)

Bowditch, A, *Working for the Great Western* (Great Western Echo, Summer 1988, Winter 1988, Spring 1989)

Buchanan, C A, *The Bridgwater & Taunton Canal* (Somerset Industrial Archaeological Survey No 1, 1984)

Clark, R H, *An Historical Survey of Selected Great Western Stations* Vols 1–3 (Oxford Publishing Company, various dates)

Clinker, C R, *Closed Stations & Goods Depots* (Avon Anglia, 1978)

Cooke, R A, *Track Layout Diagrams of the GWR & BR WR* (Sections 15–17) (R A Cooke, various dates)

Hadfield, C, *The Canals of South West England* (David & Charles, 1967)

Hateley, R, *Industrial Locomotives of South Western England* (Industrial Railway Society, 1977)

Lyons, E, *An Historical Survey of Great Western Engine Sheds 1947* (Oxford Publishing Company, 1972)

Lyons, E; Mountford, E, *An Historical Survey of Great Western Engines Sheds 1837–1947* (Oxford Publishing Company, 1979)

MacDermot, E T; Clinker, C R; Nock, O S, *History of the Great Western Railway* (Ian Allan, 1964–1967)

Maggs, C G, *The Taunton to Barnstaple Line* (Oakwood Press, 1980)

Maggs, C G, *GWR Principal Stations* (Ian Allan, 1987)

Morris, J, *Taunton* (Signalling Record Society Newsletter No 36, January 1976)

Murless, B J, *Bridgwater Docks & the River Parrett* (Somerset County Library, 1983)

Nock, O S, *Historic Railway Disasters* (Ian Allan, 1983)

Popplewell, L A, *A Gazetteer of the Railway Contractors & Engineers of the West Country 1830–1914* (Mellegen Press, 1983)

Potts, C R, *An Historical Survey of Great Western Stations* Vol 4 (Oxford Publishing Company, 1985)

Railway Correspondence & Travel Society, *Locomotives of the Great Western Railway* (RCTS, 1952–1974)

Rolt, L T C, *Red for Danger* (Pan Books, 1960)

Thomas, D St J, *A Regional History of the Railways of Great Britain, Vol 1: The West Country* (David & Charles, 1981)

Toulmin, J, *History of Taunton* (C G Webb, 1874)

Vaughan, A, *A Pictorial Record of Great Western Architecture* (Oxford Publishing Company, 1977)

Magazines: *Engineering; Great Western Railway Magazine; Illustrated London News; Railway Magazine; Trains Illustrated*
Newspapers: *Somerset County Gazette; Taunton Courier*

Acknowledgements

Grateful acknowledgement is due to Roger Venning who originated the idea of this book, carried out some of the research and provided many photographs.

Thanks are also due to Clive Bousfield, Alec & Simon Bowditch, Bob Chudleigh, Peter Doel, the late Bob Franklin, Jack Gardner, T Giannou, Tony Harvey, E J M Hayward, the late J F King, M Reynolds, Pursey Short and D R Steggles who all gave considerable help.

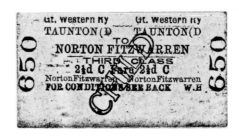